EASY GARDENS
A Weed Eater Book
Elvin McDonald

Illustrated by Phoebe Gaughan

Dorison House Publishers, Inc.
Cambridge / New York

Published by Dorison House Publishers, Inc.
183 Madison Avenue, New York, N.Y. 10016

ISBN:0-916752-20-8
Library of Congress Catalog Card Number: 77-89551
Manufactured in the United States of America

Contents

How to Have a No-Sweat, Weed-Free Garden

Energy—we save it, we use it, we waste it. And at no time in history have so many of us been concerned about the efficient use of energy—as individuals, as a nation, and as members of the global family of man.

At a national and international level, all of this may seem overwhelming, but as individuals each of us can do something about saving energy and making the most of our own resources in order to live longer, better, happier, and more productively.

Since natural energy is so deeply rooted in plants and the nurturing elements they need in order to grow and make the world better, gardening is one way that each of us can derive great personal satisfaction in our lives, at the same time we help improve the environment at large.

Unfortunately, gardening has not always been considered a totally pleasurable activity and in this fact lies the inspiration for this book. Consider, for example, the homeowner (maybe you) who has been faced with getting on his or her hands and knees to pull or dig the grass and weeds away from sidewalks, fences, trees and other hard-to-reach areas that a metal blade trimmer couldn't touch. (And even if it could, what about those blisters that are a typical side-effect of using hand-powered trimming shears?)

The good news is that there is now a popular product on the market that eliminates this back-breaking work—the monofilament line string trimmer which uses specially-treated nylon cord to cut grass and weeds. The concept was conceived and developed by a Houston businessman, George C. Ballas, who has said, "I got the idea at an automatic car-wash one day as I watched the nylon brushes spin over my car. I noticed that at high speeds the nylon strands stood out as stiff as bristles, yet were flexible enough to reach into cracks and other irregular surfaces, cleaning the car without damaging the body."

Ballas decided the same concept might work to trim grass around trees. He figured that the spinning nylon would be stiff enough to cut grass and weeds, yet flexible enough to reach in and out of areas that metal blades couldn't touch, such as around tree trunks and along sidewalks and fences.

With the idea in mind, Ballas went to his trash bin and retrieved an empty popcorn can, punched holes in it and threaded the holes with nylon fishing line. Then he removed the blade from his lawn edger, bolted the contraption in place and tried it out. It worked just long enough for Ballas to see that the spinning nylon cord tore the grass away from the tree trunk—without damaging the bark. And that is exactly what he had hoped it would do.

Ballas put his idea to work and patented it. In 1972 he formed Weed Eater, Inc., and marketed the first string trimmer, which was a rather heavy, gasoline-powered unit designed for commercial use. Consumer demand for the product did not come until about April 1973 when Weed Eater introduced the first lightweight electric unit, the Needie, which has since revolutionized lawn care and general landscape maintenance.

The product's safety features (there is no metal blade and the nylon cord will not cut flesh) and its ease of use where metal blades can't reach have made the Needie an enormous success, a tool millions of owners now find as indispensable as a power mower outdoors or a vacuum cleaner indoors. The string-line trimmer also has the added attractions of being able to function as a trimmer, edger, mower and sweeper, making it literally four tools, all very much needed, for the price of one.

To understand the importance of Ballas' invention, let's look at gardening in the United States and the phenomenal changes it has undergone since the Victory gardens of World War II.

From the late 1940s until the mid 1960s, more gardens than not were new. They were the trees, shrubs, lawns and flowers we planted around the tract houses that sprung up yearly in field after field where the season before potatoes, wheat or citrus might have grown.

Gardening in these circumstances was a terrific challenge. A few people loved it, but a lot of us decided after a few years that our idea of leisure-time activity was not spending every weekend wild-eyed and sweaty trying to create a Versailles—or at the very least, maintaining a decent front lawn so as not to fall below neighborhood standards.

In fact, by the late 1960s so many of us had decided that gardening was more pain than pleasure that the industry associated with it went into decline. Old mail-order seed and nursery companies went out of business or merged, as did the suppliers of power equipment such as lawn mowers and garden tractors. Two longtime favorite gardening magazines folded. Book publishers reduced or eliminated entirely their lists of gardening titles.

This change in attitude about gardening represented a great deal more than a desire to escape the work associated with it. With a growing awareness and concern about ecology and the environment, it was hard to muster up much enthusiasm for getting the dandelions out of your front lawn when any intimate contact with nature only sharpened your worries about pollution—in the air and from pesticides. Or made you ponder the

Computer Age and its effects on you, your family—and the whole world.

Besides, what was an overpopulation of dandelions or bugs on your roses, compared to an overpopulation of people? It was enough just trying to cope with the pill, long hair, riots, pot, runaway inflation, and unemployment. If all of this were not enough, there was also a boom in divorce, marriage without license, and women's liberation.

We will never know for sure when the change came, but the oil-energy crisis of 1973 may well have been the catalyst that turned us into a nation of gardeners. Since that time there has been a dramatic change in our attitude about growing plants. Gardening has not only become The Thing To Do, we no longer think of it as drudgery, but as a sport, as good therapy and as a means of survival both emotionally and physically.

Gardening is remarkable because it is a sport in which anyone of any age almost anywhere can participate. It takes only one plant in a pot on your windowsill to experience the wonders of nature—new green leaves, buds that turn into beautiful flowers and the good smell of moist earth.

And, if you're one of some 40 million Americans who admits that fear of trying is what keeps you from growing a garden, give yourself and nature a break. It's true, some people are born with a green thumb, but mostly it's something we acquire with experience. It makes little difference whether you start with a foliage plant in your living room or a new lawn to carpet your front yard. What is important is that you learn the basic needs of a single plant and succeed with it. Then, step-by-step you'll learn to grow almost anything in the world—for beauty, food, shade, wind protection, or fragrance.

On the other hand, if you're one of the majority of Americans already caught up in the sport of gardening, reading this book can improve your game. Use it as a source for new ideas about growing and enjoying plants in and around your home and as a refresher course to the basics.

We hope you will think of this not so much as a book about gardening, but as an introduction to a better way of life, a natural way of coping with such very real problems as stress and anxiety, frustration and anger, loneliness and the dehumanizing effects of the society in which we live.

Who you are and where you live will determine the kind of garden you grow. If you're a know-nothing beginner, take it easy. Start with a few failsafe plants that are sure confidence builders. If your thumb has gotten jaded from attempts at growing too many plants in your yard, simplify. The philosophy we share in the pages that follow is this: Gardening is for everyone, it is fun and it should be as hassle-free as possible.

Elvin McDonald
New York City

The Overview: How to Put a String-Line Trimmer to Work in Your Lawn and Garden

The monofilament string-line trimmer is one of those rare inventions that promises and delivers something that can simplify and improve the life quality of millions of people. By comparison to gimmicks and gadgets which tend to serve non-existent or trumped-up needs, it is a serious appliance that is revolutionizing the lawn and garden power equipment business.

Obviously, when a simple, inexpensive tool or other product exerts this kind of influence on a giant industry, it is time to take notice, which is what this book is all about. And to get a clear overview of how best to use a string-line trimmer in home landscapes of all sizes—from plots measured in square feet to acreages—we went directly to the man who invented it, George Ballas.

The Ballas home in Houston is surrounded by three acres of lawns, trees, shrubs, and flowerbeds. George says, "I get a lot of pleasure out of mowing grass but always hated the trim work. Maybe I was a little compulsive about having a place that looked neat and manicured but at the time I created the first string-line trimmer I was spending most of every Saturday and Sunday edging and trimming.

"When I realized I had found a quick and easy way to trim around trees, culverts, posts, flowerbeds, in ditches and valleys, I was sure that countless other homeowners would be just as thankful to have such a convenience as I was."

George was right, of course, and today his files bulge with letters of appreciation that he receives from enthusiastic users of the Weed Eater line of string-line trimmers all over the world. Based on his own experiences and those of satisfied customers, George makes these general and specific recommendations:

For edging chores of all kinds, nothing equals the ease and efficiency of a string-line trimmer. Now you can put up all the picket fences and flowerbeds you want without fear of time-consuming and repetitive hard work. Along the ragged edges of a blacktop or gravel driveway, for example, regular edgers can't be used at all, yet a Weed Eater product such as the Needie will scalp cleanly along the edges in minutes.

Other edging problems you can solve with a string-line trimmer in-

Edging a walk   *Trimming a picket fence*

clude these: around concrete drainage gutters, air conditioner compression units, posts (fence, clothesline, mailbox, gas or electric barbecue grills), walls and fences of all kinds, lawn furniture, steps, sidewalks, all outbuildings, and flowerbeds.

Hand trimming around trees was a particular nuisance for George since more than 200 are scattered in his lawn. With a string-line trimmer, he recommends this procedure: Keeping the tree to your right side, scalp a ring around the tree trunk; come out 18'' to 36'' depending on the size of the tree. Then reverse direction, so the tree will be on your left, and complete the scalp, ending up with a clean circle, up to 3' in diameter around the trunk. Once you scalp around a tree, you have to do it only two or three times a year, compared to as often as once a week with old-fashioned edging methods.

A string-line trimmer will also do a fantastic job in tidying up the edges of ponds, lakes, streams, and around docks and decks. Around drainage gutters you can even cut grass that is sticking out of water in a ditch—something not possible with any other power or hand tool.

By proper spacing of flowers and shrubs, you can keep the ground between scalped and free of weeds without the trouble and expense of applying mulches or chemicals. The smaller Weed Eater units have a 7'' cut and can be used between plants or shrubs spaced 9'' or more apart; for a unit with an 18'' cut, George suggests spacing plants at least 20'' apart in all directions. By this approach, it is possible to use a string-line trimmer instead of a hoe for cleaning out flower, vegetable, and herb gardens, not to mention home orchards and vineyards.

Where ground cover such as periwinkle, pachysandra, or English ivy meets the lawn, turn the Weed Eater unit on its side for a neat trim, or cut once with the metal blade attachment; maintenance for the balance of the year will be a snap.

The larger model Weed Eater string-line trimmers, those with a 15'' cut and above, are available in gas or electric models. These have at least four functions: trimming, edging, mowing, and sweeping. Many owners of small lawns, both in North America and Europe, are using string-line trimmers of this size for all yard maintenance; they have found that no mower and no other type of edger is necessary. For sweeping, one of these units air-cleans walkways instantly, eliminating any need for wielding a broom.

Scalping around a tree   Trimming around or on black top

Perhaps one of the greatest benefits of using a string-line trimmer for all edging/trimming chores around a property is that it eliminates the hazards of power lawn mowers. As George points out, ''Trimming with a power mower where it shouldn't be used is a prime cause of accidents—any place where rocks, wire coat hangers, nails, or other debris are likely to be lodged. Rotary mowers tend to stir them up so that they can become lethal missiles. Young people, or anyone who has small children around, owe it

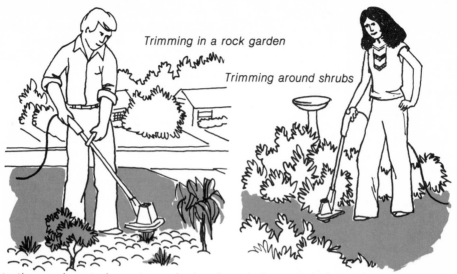

Trimming in a rock garden

Trimming around shrubs

to themselves to be extremely cautious in how and where they use a power mower.''

Another hazard a string-line trimmer can eliminate is the possibility of snakebite. To illustrate, George recalls how he once hired a man to clean out the weeds and grass between the support roots of his large trees. ''Not ten minutes after he started working he was bitten by a copperhead. Thank God the man wasn't killed. Unfortunately, I never did get the rest of the weeds cleared from around the trees—at least not until I invented an easy, safe way to do it.''

The larger-size Weed Eater units with gasoline engines are recommended for large properties, especially rural ones. Use the optional brush blade, a metal attachment, for clearing heavy undergrowth, then you can keep the area clean with the string line. The optional saw blade attachment for these units will cut level with the ground, or even below, and up to an 8'' trunk diameter. By comparison, a chain saw can't cut level with the ground and is therefore far less satisfactory for this kind of clearing work.

For the initial shaping-up of a property, so that it can be easily and quickly maintained in the future with a string-line trimmer, George recommends the non-growing season. ''The fall and winter months, even into early spring, are ideal for all initial scalping work around trees or other obstructions in a lawn area. I like to spread this kind of work over a period of three or four months. Once you get circles scalped around trees, posts, bushes, and 5'' or 6'' back from fences, walls, and steps, you can do an average place in 30 minutes and keep it neat and manicured looking year 'round without ever feeling that you are some kind of yard slave.''

Trimming around a tree

Trimming around a flower bed

Trimming ivy

Trimming around a lake or pond

Select the Right Nylon Line Trimmer for Your Job

There is a wide variety of trimmers and trimmer/edgers that carry the Weed Eater brand name. Each is designed to do a particular job or group of jobs. The chart below is a guide to help you select the correct tool for your needs.

Motor Rating	Approximate Cutting Path	Approximate Weight	Typical Uses
Battery	7½''	7 lbs.	Light trimming where extension cord is inconvenient.
1.5 amps	8''	2 lbs.	Light grass trimming only. Small patio-size lawns.
2 amps	10''	3½ lbs.	Trimming grass and light weeds. Medium-to-small lawns.
4-6 amps	16''	8 lbs.	Trimming, edging, mowing and sweeping. Versatile tools for most lawns.
2-cycle, 14-22cc gas engine	16''	10-12 lbs.	Trimming, edging, mowing and sweeping on any size lawn or estate.
2-cycle, 37-85cc gas engine	17-21''	13-25 lbs.	Professional model tools. Trimming, edging, mowing and sweeping. Some models accommodate brush and saw blades.

Part 1
Garden to Suit Yourself

Since infinite variables help to determine the kind of garden that will be right for you, the purpose of this chapter is to suggest some of the possibilities. Besides your own personal preferences, the three main points to consider are space, light, and climate (either natural or man-made).

More and more in the future, where and how we live is going to be influenced by the kinds of plants and gardens we want to grow. As recently as the early 1970s, houses and apartments were built or chosen entirely to meet the requirements of the human occupants. The realization that living, thriving plants are not accessories or knick-knacks, but necessities vital to human happiness and a sense of well-being, means that consideration for their basic needs now ranks second only to our own.

But for now, your present surroundings will determine the opportunities and limitations of your gardening life. So, in deciding what kind of garden you want, consider:

1. The basic needs of plants and your ability to provide them.
2. The amount of space and time you can devote to them.
3. The type of plant or garden that you long for the most.

Basic Needs of Plants

The conditions a plant requires in order to thrive and bear the foliage, flowers, or fruit we expect of it are not all that different from own own. Plants need light, water, nutrients, tolerable temperatures, and protection from pests and disease. Of these, light and temperature are the important factors that determine whether or not you will be able to grow a particular plant. Water, nutrients, and protection from pests and disease are relatively easy to provide.

Light. Whether you want to grow a plant indoors or outdoors, it will need a certain amount of light in order to thrive. The range or quality of light varies from full sun to full shade, with intermediate stops at semisunny and semishady. The duration of any one of these kinds of light determines its effect on plants.

Full sun describes a place either indoors or outdoors that receives the direct rays of sunlight for more than a half day.

Semisunny describes a place either indoors or outdoors that receives the direct rays of sunlight for three hours up to a half day.

Semishady describes a place either indoors or outdoors that receives the direct rays of sunlight for one to three hours a day.

Full shade describes a place either indoors or outdoors that receives less than an hour of direct sunlight a day, but light bright enough for you to read by comfortably.

Throughout this book, the light needs of the plants are specified. In practice, most plants will adapt one step up or down from the optimum; for example, if the best light for a plant is semisunny, it will probably also grow acceptably in full sun or semishade; or, if semishade is the optimum, semisun or full shade will be acceptable. Relatively few plants will grow acceptably in a broader range; in other words, plants that need full sun are seldom able to thrive in semishade, and by the same token, a shade-loving plant will seldom be able to adapt to full sun.

Climate. The plants we grow have an incredibly broad tolerance of temperatures—from subzero to 100°F or more. A plant's natural habitat determines not only the maximum highs and lows it can tolerate, but also the seasonal changes required for survival. The basic categories suggested here are intended as general guidelines; the needs of specific plants are given throughout this book.

Temperate-climate plants are accustomed to a definite seasonal timetable that is controlled primarily by changes in temperature. They grow actively in temperatures above freezing. When temperatures drop below 32°F, they go into a state of dormancy. Relatively few plants that originate in a temperate climate are able to adapt to a climate where freezing temperatures do not occur annually.

Tropical-climate plants are accustomed to growing all year where temperatures seldom if ever reach as low as 32°F. They, too, go through annual periods of dormancy or semidormancy, but instead of this being triggered by freezing, it is usually the result of a dry season which may or may not be accompanied by relative cold or heat that is inhospitable to active growth. The better your knowledge of the world's geography and varied climates, the better gardener you will be.

If you live in a temperate climate, where freezing temperatures occur, you can grow almost any tropical plant outdoors in warm weather and indoors at any time when there is danger of freezing. However, if the plant you want to grow originated in a tropical rain forest, it will need at least 40% humidity indoors during the winter heating season.

On the other hand, if you live in a tropical climate, relatively few plants that hail from temperate parts of the world can be cultivated because they cannot survive without an annual rest induced by freezing temperatures. Exceptions to this general rule are given for specific plants throughout this book. For example, certain roses and daffodils will grow in the tropics, others will grow a season or two and then go into decline. To grow tulips and hyacinths in the deep South, you will have to chill the bulbs in the vegetable crisper of your refrigerator (at about 40-45°F) from October to December, then plant them outdoors.

If you are by nature adventuresome, you may want to experiment with tropical plants in a temperate climate or vice versa. While the life of a plant is at stake, this is the way we discover new horizons in gardening. Camellias, for example, thrive in protected corners of gardens far north of where they are generally thought to grow. And, by experimenting with many different tulips, you may discover certain varieties that will return and bloom year after year in a warm climate.

Type of Dwelling

Besides the climate where you live and your individual personality, the size and type of dwelling is also influential in determining the right garden for you. There are infinite variables, but in the simplest terms, we live either in houses or apartments, with or without space outdoors for growing plants.

Whether you live in a one-room efficiency or a ramble of many rooms, you can grow plants indoors. If there is not sufficient natural light, grow plants in artificial light.

Space to grow plants outdoors can vary from a single window box to acreage. If lack of space outdoors cramps your style as a gardener, involvement in a community gardening project may be the answer. If, for example, you want to grow vegetables but have no outdoor garden, or your gardening space outdoors is too heavily shaded by trees or buildings to grow vegetables, then you may be able to sign up for a plot within a community vegetable garden. If you have no suitable place to garden outdoors, but crave the experience of nurturing flowers, trees, or shrubs, you can become a volunteer gardener for almost any public garden—perhaps a community beautification project, plantings around a church or school, or the landscape of a botanical garden.

Obviously, the type of dwelling in which you live influences how you garden, and may impose limitations. However, as you grow older and wiser, your gardening and plant preferences can have a strong and positive influence on the type of dwelling in which you choose to live. My dwellings over these first forty years of my life have run the gamut from one-room apartments in cities to roomy country houses sited on hundreds of acres of land.

Now I get enormous pleasure out of dreaming about my next dwelling and how it will be shaped and sited to suit the kind of garden I want to grow. And, while I love all plants, I have always lived in temperate climates. I am looking forward to the time when I can live in a balmy clime where all of my favorite tropicals can grow outdoors naturally. I know also that my greatest love is for container gardening indoors and outdoors, so the landscape of my dreams takes this into account. For acres of trees, shrubs, lawns, ground covers, and hedges I'll go to public places unless I can afford a gardener. And, when I'm very old, I think some highly sophisticated form of what we call a fluorescent-light garden will make me happy.

This philosophy of gardening-to-suit-yourself will be faultless if you let your garden change as you do. If your garden does not give you great pleasure, something is wrong. Mild enthusiasm will not make you a devotee of gardening, but if you know you love plants, there is absolutely some kind of horticultural pursuit that is uniquely suited to your emotional and physical needs. Some people are generalists, others can't be happy without specialization. Having always grown at least 200 different kinds of plants at any given time, I am beginning to think I would like to concentrate on fewer at any given time in order to pay more attention to their individual needs.

And I'd like to have the sense of making a real collection of one genus of plants. I met recently a woman in Texas who grows only hoyas, what once was known as the wax-plant; she has more different varieties than anyone else in the world. And, coincidentally, I know a man in Texas who has more species and varieties of lithops (living stones) than any major botanical garden. I admire these individuals' devotion to one kind of plant. It has a sense of order and discipline that seems especially welcome in today's world.

Making the Right Choice

The kind of garden that is right for you is influenced by many highly variable factors, but if you think about them one at a time, your decision will at least be informed and studied.

Type of growth you want, for example: vegetables and herbs for gourmet cooking; trees and shrubs for shade, privacy, windbreak, flowers, berries, fruit, interesting bark; flowers for fragrance, cutting, drying; a lawn to set off your house, complement flower and shrubbery borders, provide a soft, living carpet on which to play; or indoor plants for foliage, flowers, and sweet scents in the rooms where you live.

Considerations of climate interrelate with the type of growth you want. Familiarize yourself with the climate where you live; determine the maximum-minimum annual temperatures, annual rainfall, and prevailing winds. Then study the micro-climates that exist inside and all around your dwelling. If a south-facing window is shaded by a big evergreen tree, it will not receive enough light for sun-loving plants. On the other hand, if that tree is deciduous, from the time it loses its leaves in autumn until green-up time the following spring, the window will be sunny.

Outdoors, a chance or intentional grouping of rocks might shield a planting pocket from the coldest winter winds and turn it into an unseasonably warm micro-climate. The better you know these little climates, the better gardener you will be.

Level of gardening experience is a vital consideration. Start small, diversify slowly—and if it all gets to be too much for you, don't hesitate to cut back, either literally or figuratively.

Amount of time and money you wish or can afford to invest in gardening helps determine what is right. Fortunately, money is not a necessity, but making a commitment of time and energy sufficient to nurture your garden well is an essential.

The size and location of a gardening space, whether it is indoors or outdoors, affects the kind of garden that will be right for you—within the framework of the four considerations previously suggested. If, for example, the space is small, you can be happy with miniature, dwarf, or naturally slow-growing plants. On the other hand, large, rapid-growing plants in that same space won't please you for long nor will they thrive indefinitely in increasingly crowded quarters.

The purpose of the garden is a consideration worth some soul searching. You may garden for food or protection from the elements, but the greater rewards beyond these basics are more abstract. Think in terms of what kind of garden is the epitome of beauty—to you. Plants and gardens are living sensualities with individual and fascinating characteristics. If their ever-changing forms, textures, colors, and fragrances give you pleasure, then you will have discovered what gardening is really all about.

1 • Plan Before Planting
(And What To Do If You Didn't)

Although it's possible to grow a yard filled with fantastic plants without ever giving much thought to the over-all design, the most totally satisfying gardens usually begin on paper. As anyone who has gardened for long knows, it is a lot easier to transplant trees and shrubs with an eraser than with a spade. An accurate plot plan will also help you to see the measured relationships of everything on your property.

Essentially what you'll need to do a plan of your yard or garden are pencils, an eraser, paper, and a ruler. I like to use 24'' x 36'' graph paper, a pad of tracing paper the same size, a T-square, triangle, and compass. For outdoor measuring, you'll need a 100' tapemeasure—and someone to hold the other end.

If you can locate a survey or deed map, you will save hours of measuring, especially on a large property. This should be on file at your city hall, county courthouse, bank, mortgage, or title company. For a hillside site, you will need a contour map on which an engineer will have indicated contours in measurements of 1', 2', 5', or 10'.

Once you have all of these supplies—and a helper—you're ready to go outdoors and start measuring. Depending on the size of your graph paper and your property, determine what scale to use. If the total area is a half acre or less you might use 1/4'' to equal 1', but on larger properties I suggest letting 1'' equal 10' or 20'.

At this stage I use masking tape to attach a large sheet of graph paper on a drafting board (from an art supply store) so that outdoors I have a solid surface on which to write and the wind doesn't disturb my work. The purpose of measuring is to determine the exact location of all major trees, shrubs, lawns or other planted areas, plus the house, other buildings, fences, sidewalks, power lines, poles, easements, and rights-of-way.

The way I do this on a property that has lots of trees and shrubs is to indicate them as masses rather than individuals. It will help, however, to indicate the trunk as well as approximate branch spread of any large trees.

Once you have finished measuring, the real fun of planning can begin. If you're very neat and organized, the notes and sketches you made outdoors may constitute a satisfactory working plan; personally, I usually have to re-draw everything before proceeding. In either case, the next step is to put a sheet of tracing paper over the master plan, then begin sketching. By using the tracing paper as an overlay, you can try out an endless variety of ideas without disturbing the master plan.

One-story ranch or provincial. *The landscape plan for this one-story ranch or provincial features curved edges for the lawn—to reduce the amount of lawn maintenance. 1. English ivy as a low hedge. Use Boston ivy on north-facing wall. 2.-3. Andorra juniper, Mugho pine or Pfitzer juniper. 4. A row of Mugho pines or globe arborvitae along the walk to the front door. Or, plant spring bulbs followed by summer annuals interplanted with chrysanthemums and dwarf hardy asters. 5. Savins or Andorra juniper. 6. Spring-flowering bulbs and summer annuals followed by hardy chrysanthemums and dwarf hardy asters. 7. Pin oak, Norway maple or European linden. 8. Espalier tomatoes or grapevines. 9. Vegetable garden. 10. All red plum tree, redbud, or Lilliputian magnolia. 11. Perennial border. 12. Apple or cherry tree, or Sunburst locust. 13. Same as 11, but keep tall plants away from front view of the espaliers against the fence. 14. Dwarf apples or pears espaliered on fence. 15. Dwarf bush cherries, flowering crab apple or a flowering peach tree. 16. Rose garden or a planting of evergreens. 17.-18. Spring-flowering bulbs followed by summer annual flowers. Interplant some hardy mums or asters for fall color. 19. Sunburst locust, Russian olive or paper white birch.*

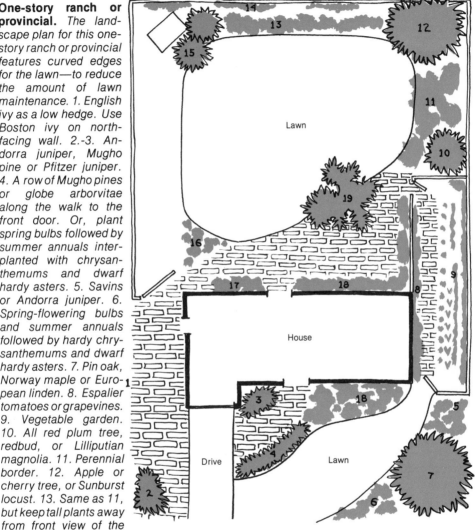

When you have completed a new master plan, transfer it from the tracing paper to a clean sheet of graph paper, and then have two or three copies made—one to keep clean indoors, another you can take into the garden to guide your work, and possibly a third to carry with you when you go shopping for plant materials or building supplies.

Although a total landscape plan may seem overwhelming at the outset, it needn't be if you divide it into smaller parts. Since most landscapes immediately surrounding a dwelling consist of the public garden or access area, the living or private area, and the service area, I recommend using these three divisions. Obviously, in the end they all have to work together, but as a design problem, it's much easier to tackle one basic area at a time.

One of the chief advantages of putting all of this effort into developing a master plan is that it will help you spot plant and landscaping problems or mistakes. And in gardening, like most endeavors, knowing what the problem is constitutes at least half of the battle; one or more solutions will likely come to mind. For example, consider these situations:

Steep bank. Do you have a patch of lawn that is a constant annoyance to mow because the ground slopes steeply? Replace the grass with a low-upkeep ground cover like pachysandra, English ivy, or Vinca minor. Or you can turn the area into a fascinating rock garden, knowing all the while that a string-line trimmer will help you keep it tidy with hardly any effort.

Well-placed walkways. Are you trying to maintain lawn or flowers where people—your own spouse and children—insist on beating a path? Better to join them; put down an attractive walkway such as flagstone, brick, or wood rounds.

Privacy for play. The children's play yard should be on view from a vantage point in the house where it is most convenient for someone to supervise. But if it's in full view of your neighbor's outdoor living room, or exposed to the street, give everybody a break and plant a nice hedge of privet, hemlock, or yew.

Driveway. If your driveway looks too stark or utilitarian, try bordering it with neat dwarf evergreens, or rows of peonies or daylilies.

Camouflage storage. A tool shed on your property can do wonders for taking clutter out of the garage—but most prefabricated storage units are ugly in the landscape. Screen from view with tall evergreens. Plant annuals or perennials in front for flowers in season.

Border. To give a neat appearance, control weeds and give wheel room for your power mower, edge flower beds and borders with bricks or flat flagstones set flush with the soil surface. Do the final trimming—which makes the difference between a nice-looking yard and a beautiful garden—with a string-line trimmer.

Drought-tolerant plantings for a sloping lot. *In a dry year the plant materials suggested in this plan will do exceptionally well. They are also recommended for semi-arid climates. 1. Ginkgo or Norway Maple. 2. Redbud trees. 3. Savins juniper. 4. Red barberry. 5. Tamarix shrub. 6. Redmond linden tree. 7. Hybrid lilacs. 8. Honeysuckle bushes. 9. Barberry shrubs. 10. A border of sedums. 11. Golden elder or variegated weigela. 12. Potentilla. 13. Brownell floribunda roses. 14. Vinca minor (periwinkle). 15. Golden-rain tree. 16. Crape-myrtle shrubs. 17. Mugho pines. 18. Norway maple or ginkgo. 19. Fragrant viburnum. 20. Russian olive tree. 21. Variegated weigela. 22. Amur cork tree. 23. Crownvetch or Hall's honeysuckle. 24. Shademaster locust tree. 25. Kazan firethorn shrub. 26. Russian olive trees. 27. Paper white birch tree. 28. Blueberry bushes.*

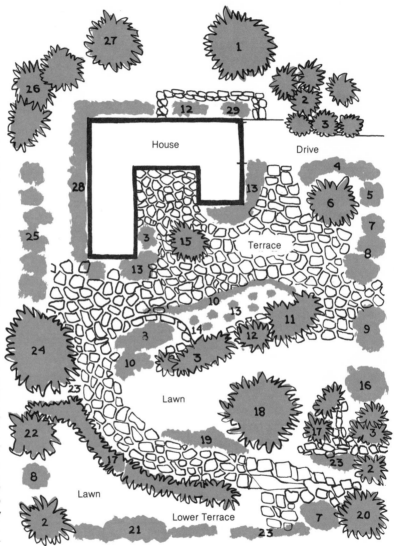

Symmetrical balance

The art of framing. Whether it is your front door as viewed from the street or a vista from some window inside your home, take advantage of plant materials for framing an attractive view.

Add dimension. Sometimes the architectural detail of a trellis or arbor adds that perfect finishing touch to a landscape that is otherwise beautiful. Vines can also be trained on the uprights as privacy screening, or overhead for quick, pleasant shading.

Entryways. Try to use naturally neat evergreens to frame your door-way. They give a presentable appearance without backbreaking upkeep, and also give encouraging green color in winter.

Asymmetrical balance

New dimension for a small lot. *The idea here is to make a narrow lot look wide. 1. Hedge of American arborvitae, Austrian pine, or Norway spruce. 2. Spring-flowering bulbs followed by annual flowers. A foundation planting of Emerald euonymus, Mugho pines or Clavey's dwarf honeysuckle would look good here. 3. Spreading yew, interplanted each summer with impatiens, tuberous-rooted begonias, and caladiums for color in the shade. 4. Kazan firethorn, white snowball, or flowering quince. 5. Could be same as 1, or put in English ivy trimmed, or clipped spreading yew. 6. Flowering crab apple, dogwood or redbud, underplanted with English ivy. 7. Emerald euonymus, potentilla or dwarf crape-myrtle. 8. Kazan firethorn trained or espaliered on a 6' to 8' trellis for privacy. 9. Dwarf crape-myrtle or one of the potentillas. 10. Same as 8. For less formal effect, use Persian lilac, althea, crape-myrtle, or highbush cranberry. 11. Redbud, flowering peach, flowering crab apple, or dogwood. 12. Russian olive, hybrid elm or mountain-ash. 13. Spring bulbs overplanted with hybrid petunias in summer. 14. Dogwood, redbud or flowering crab apple. 15. Flowering shrubs such as the spireas, lilacs, dwarf crape-myrtle, golden mockorange, Chinese beauty bush, weigela, butterfly bush and forsythia. 16. Hedge of blueberries, gooseberries, raspberries or a hedge of Chinese elm. Amur River privet or Tatarian honeysuckle. 17. Vegetable garden. Train grapevines or tomatoes on fence. 18. Apple, cherry, pin oak, or Sunburst locust tree. 19. Three fruit trees or flowering crab apples. 20. Bush cherries, flowering quince, or flowering shrubs as suggested for 15 and 16. 21. Rose garden. 22. Perennial flower garden. 23. Althea, flowering crab apple, dogwood, redbud or white birch clump, underplanted with spring-flowering bulbs and annual flowers. 24. European linden or Sunburst locust.*

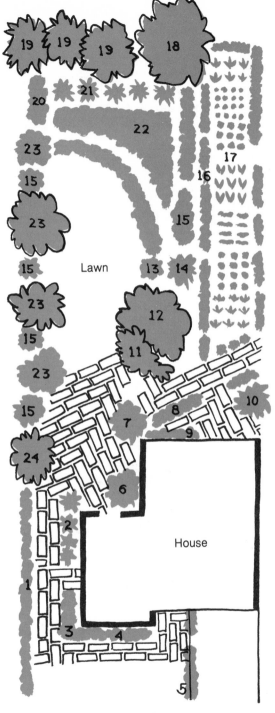

Little climates. Around your garden you will find microclimates—little pockets where temperatures are likely to be colder, or warmer, at any given moment than in other areas. You can make these work to your advantage. For instance, crocus planted at the base of a warm wall will bloom much earlier than those in the open garden.

Hidden but convenient. Use compact evergreen shrubs or ornamental fencing to screen unsightly necessities in your garden—trash cans, for instance.

Before you start sketching your master plan, study the suggested planting designs included in this chapter. These are filled with proven good ideas for front yards and foundation plantings, backyards and patios. In addition, there is one highly adaptable plan for coping when you have acreage.

The Best Laid Plans ...

Before you start planting in either a new or old garden, it pays to know some down-to-earth facts about your soil. No matter how vigorous your plants may be when you buy them, their ultimate success depends on the soil in which they are planted.

A common mistake is to assume that the application of a heavy dose of fertilizer makes a good soil. There is much more to it. Good garden soil should be of a texture that will hold plants securely in place, release plant foods to the roots slowly over a long period, and retain moisture like a

Landscape areas

sponge, while at the same time allowing any surplus water to drain off rapidly.

In beds and borders soil may usually be improved without removing it, by adding fertilizer and sphagnum peat moss; but if very poor—such as almost pure sand or very heavy clay—it is more satisfactory to take it out entirely to the depth of a foot or more and replace it with good loam or a mixture of approximately 1/3 sand, 1/3 clay loam, and 1/3 humus such as moist sphagnum peat moss or well-rotted compost. Lime should be added if the soil is acid and a complete fertilizer applied in accordance with the recommendations on the package.

Generally speaking, soils in the Eastern United States must be amended periodically with lime to bring the pH (the measure of acidity) up to the neutral range. Many plants can grow in the range pH 4 (highly acidic) to pH 9 (highly alkaline), but most plants grow best when the pH is between 6.0 (slightly acidic) to 7.5 (slightly alkaline). Soil pH can be tested easily with test kits sold by mail and at local garden centers and nurseries. The pH can be raised by adding lime, and lowered by adding either elemental sulfur, iron sulfate, or aluminum sulfate.

Sphagnum peat moss is unequalled as a soil conditioner in garden beds and borders, and as an essential ingredient in most potting soil mixtures. Well-rotted compost is equally useful, and since it is something you can make at home using organic refuse from the kitchen and the garden, instructions have been included on page 31.

Where the physical character of soil has been improved by the addition of sand or clay loam as the case may be, plus humus in the form of peat moss or compost, it should retain moisture well, yet provide good drainage of any surplus water. Few plants thrive in soggy soil. The roots of all plants (except waterlilies and other aquatics) require air as well as moisture, and without it they soon perish, no matter how rich the soil.

In addition to good drainage, plants require an adequate food supply. The chief plant food elements are nitrogen, phosphorus, and potash. Any complete fertilizer contains all three, plus very small quantities of such elements as boron and iron, mere traces of which are required for healthy plant growth. Nitrogen, which is essential in initiating new growth, produces the quickest, most easily recognized effects. But unless nitrogen is accompanied by phosphorus and potash, such growth is not normal and may eventually prove injurious to the plant's general health.

The too-frequent application of high-nitrogen fertilizer is likely to cause excessive growth of stems and foliage at the expense of flower production. Don't go too heavy on nitrogen. If plants appear unhealthy or foliage is pale or yellowish instead of healthy bright green, then an application of high-nitrogen fertilizer is probably indicated.

Gardens and lawns, when actively growing, usually require about 1" of water per week. If rainfall does not furnish this, supplemental watering is needed. One good soaking per week is much better than more frequent light sprinkles.

Most lawn and garden sprinklers apply about a quarter of an inch per hour. This can easily be checked. Place one or more tin cans or other containers with straight sides in the area to be sprinkled and measure the amount of moisture collected in one hour.

Moisture content of the soil at the time of cultivation is critical, particularly for soils with relatively large amounts of clay. Tilling a clay loam or finer-textured soil when too wet or too dry often results in large clods. At an intermediate water content the soil can usually be broken without destroying the natural structure. The proper moisture content can be determined very easily. Dig up a handful of soil. Squeeze it. If it crumbles, the moisture is right for cultivation. If it remains in a tight ball, it is too wet to disturb.

When preparing a new planting bed, I recommend a centuries-old technique known as trenching or double-digging. Here's how: Begin at one end of the area. Dig a trench 12" wide by 20" deep. Transfer this soil to the opposite end of the area to be dug. Next to the first trench, dig a second, 12" wide by 10" deep. Spade this soil into the first trench. Enrich it with compost. Dig another 10" out of the second trench and toss soil in the first one. Continue procedure to the end of the area. Soil from the first trench goes into the last trench.

Organic Gardening: The Natural Way

Those who've been at it a long time call it "organic gardening." Those younger in years or experience call it "green survival." Call it what you will, but when such earthy words as well-rotted manure, compost pile, and mulch are being bandied about at cocktail parties and, indeed, around very elegant dinner tables, it's time to take notice. Which is just exactly what a lot of people are doing nowadays.

Certain prudent gardeners have probably utilized organic methods since the very beginning of agriculture, but in modern times an awareness of the practice dates from early in this century, when Sir Albert Howard, an English agricultural advisor to the Indian state of Indore, first developed a method of farming which did not include synthetic chemicals but relied entirely upon available natural materials.

Good soil is not inert but is full of microorganisms which act upon residues of plant and animal tissue to form humus. Besides providing nutrients, humus improves the structure of the soil, making it spongy, easily permeable by air and water, and resistant to erosion.

In native forests and prairies there is a permanent state of soil fertility. All that is produced by the soil eventually dies, decays, and goes back into the soil as humus. Man and agriculture disrupt this cycle. The organic gardener perceives a balance in nature and tries to maintain it in his garden.

Diseases and pest-ridden plants are often the first symptoms of low soil fertility. Most organic gardeners use compost to maintain fertility. To start a compost program, one needs some sort of bin. This may be made of almost any inexpensive material such as waste lumber, wire, or concrete block.

A good method of composting is to put down a 5'' or 6'' layer of green matter, such as garden waste, grass clippings, weeds, then a 2'' layer of manure and a layer of rich earth, with added ground limestone and phosphate rock. Provide ventilation by placing pipes or thick stakes through the pile as it is being built and pull them out later. Keep the pile moist but not soggy. Compost can be made by this method in three months. The pile is turned at about six weeks and again at about 12 weeks. Heat in the center of the pile may reach 150°F even in the fall, a good time to begin a compost pile in most temperate zones.

What is suitable for composting? Garden residues, grass clippings, leaves, weeds with immature seeds, manure, rock particles, and household garbage (except soapy water and fats).

When most of the heat has gone out of the compost pile, a supply of earthworms is sometimes added to it. Earthworms eat soil, digest it, and condition it. Their burrows aid in aerating the soil and in water absorption, both essential.

Compost is ready to use when it is dark, rich looking, crumbly, and most of the large materials are broken down into small pieces. It may need to be screened if it is to be used in flower beds and pots (I use 1/4'' wire hardware cloth for screening compost).

A good time to apply compost is annually, about a month before planting. The soil is turned and compost is added to the top 4'' in a layer from 1'' to 3'' in thickness, with some thought as to whether the planned crop is a heavy or light feeder. However, there is no danger of putting on too heavy a layer of compost. If it is well prepared it will not burn plants, as immediately soluble chemical fertilizers may. Compost nutrients are released slowly as needed.

There are alternatives to the pile or bin method of composting. Soil fertility and conditioning can be obtained by growing a cover crop and turning it under as green manure. A nitrogen-fixing legume such as clover or vetch is a good choice for green manuring.

Sheet composting is probably the easiest way to make and use compost. In this method the materials are spread directly on the planting area and turned under with a rotary tiller.

Mulching is used by many organic gardeners. A layer of mulch material is placed around growing plants to moderate soil temperature, to decay and add fertility, to keep the soil loose and eliminate the need for cultivation, to conserve moisture and to protect ripening fruit. Some useful mulch materials are grass clippings, leaves, stones, hulls and shells, sawdust and wood chips, shredded cornstalks, straw, alfalfa, and hay.

Organic gardeners are generally opposed to the use of chlorinated hydrocarbons such as DDT for the control of pests. These hard chemicals do not deteriorate or disappear but travel up the natural food chain from insect to man. They are of a broad-spectrum type, killing off from 100 to 1,000 species of insects, some of which are beneficial, including natural predators and parasites of insects the gardener wants to eliminate. Also, harmful insects are able to develop strains resistant to hard chemicals.

Preventive measures can often head off trouble. Select seeds and plants of highly resistant varieties. Destroy diseased plants by burning or placing them deep in the hot center of a compost pile. Avoid monoculture; in other words, don't grow your tomatoes in exactly the same plot of ground year after year. Rotation of crops helps discourage diseases.

In this plan consider companion planting—the growing of different species in close proximity for the benefit of one of them. Chives planted among roses tend to keep aphids away. Some growers have found that marigolds planted with beans prevent Mexican bean beetle infestation. At the end of this chapter is a list of plants which similarly help each other.

If pests have already invaded, one still need not use hard chemicals. Make use of a pest's natural enemies. Ladybugs can be purchased by the gallon for control of aphids, mites, and scale insects. The trichogramma, a parasitic wasp, eats the eggs of many moths and butterflies which are leaf-eaters in their larval stage.

Birds may be encouraged to help with pest control by feeding them and providing them with water and nesting materials during seasons when insects are not plentiful. Toads are also allies of the gardener. They like a shallow pan filled with water and a toad house made by breaking a small hole in a clay flowerpot and turning it upside down in a cool, shaded, moist place.

Some gardeners have successfully used insect disease to control pests. For instance, Bacillus thuringiensis is effective against some 60 or more insect pests. It is highly selective and will not harm beneficial insects; it is nontoxic to humans and warm-blooded animals.

Dry powders or dusts desiccate and thus kill pests. Some effective dusts are lime, talc, silica, and diatomaceous earth. Ground green shallot onions mixed with water in equal parts are effective against aphids. Hot-pepper spray eliminates cabbage worms. Organic gardeners also approve pyrethrum, ryania, and rotenone, all of which are plant-derived, natural pesticides.

For the gardener who would avoid poison sprays and synthetic fertilizers, natural organic materials are available.

The biodynamic gardeners follow organic methods but use more sophisticated techniques. Compost preparation is scientifically controlled with exact mixtures being made for specific situations. The biodynamic gardener also takes into account compatible and companion plantings, as well as the succession of crops by those whose soil needs complement each other. For instance, a plant which needs a high nitrogen content is rotated with one which replaces nitrogen.

Companion and compatible plantings are also among the weapons in the organic gardener's arsenal. Following are lists of plants which help each other in various ways and some which are inimical to pests. A companion plant is one that assists another plant in the control of a disease or pest, such as marigolds, asters, chrysanthemums, cosmos, and coreopsis. And most aromatic herbs also achieve this highly desirable effect. Among these are basil, anise, coriander, rosemary, and sage. Organic gardeners recommend either planting these insect-repelling flowers and herbs in the vegetable garden and annual or perennial beds, or as edging in these situations.

Companion Planting Chart

Plant	Companion	To Repel
Asparagus	Tomatoes	Asparagus beetles
Beans	Potatoes	Mexican bean beetle
	Marigolds	Mexican bean beetle
	Nasturtiums	Mexican bean beetle
Broccoli	Nasturtiums	Aphids
Cabbage	Sage	Cabbage butterfly
	Tansy	Cabbage worm and cutworms
	Tomatoes	Cabbage butterfly
	Mint	Cabbage maggot
	Rosemary	Cabbage maggot
Corn	Larkspur	Japanese beetles
	Soybeans	Japanese beetles and chinch bugs
Cucumbers	Marigolds	Cucumber beetles
	Nasturtiums	Striped cucumber beetles and squash bugs
	Radishes	Striped or spotted cucumber beetles
Grapes	Geraniums	Japanese beetles
Lettuce	Chives	Aphids
Peach tree	Garlic	Peach tree borer
Peas	Chives	Aphids
Potatoes	Beans	Colorado potato beetles
	Horseradish	Potato bugs
Roses	Geraniums	Japanese beetles
	Chives	Aphids
	Parsley	Rose beetles
	Garlic	Black spot, mildew, aphids
Squash	Radishes	Squash bugs
Any plant	Marigolds	Nematodes
Any plant	Onions	Cutworms
Any plant	Radishes	Attract root maggots; plant them as a trap crop

Part 2
The Right Plant
for the Right Place

When my sixth-grade science teacher taught us that a weed is a plant, any plant, out of place, I violently disagreed with him. I couldn't have quoted Gertrude Stein then, but I think I said, more or less, what she wrote: "A rose is a rose is a rose..."

Now, some 28 years, several gardens, and a lot of weeds later, I have to say my teacher's definition was absolutely right. A thorny rosebush planted too close to where you walk will be literally a pain in the arm—if not some other part of the anatomy—and in that sense it becomes a weed, a plant out of place.

Therefore, if you want to plant a garden that will be a growing success year after year, with the least amount of work, spend some time selecting the right plants for the right places. In fact, a lot of us who enjoy gardening know that part of the fun lies in dreaming over the seed catalogs and visiting local nurseries and garden centers just to see what's available. If you lay all of this thought about the plant materials against the plans you have drawn, perhaps as suggested earlier, your garden is bound to be a success.

The purpose of this chapter is to suggest the major kinds of plant materials from which you can choose and to suggest rewarding ways of putting them to work in your life. These categories include flowers, trees, shrubs, vines, lawns, ground covers, vegetables, herbs, fruits, berries—and house plants.

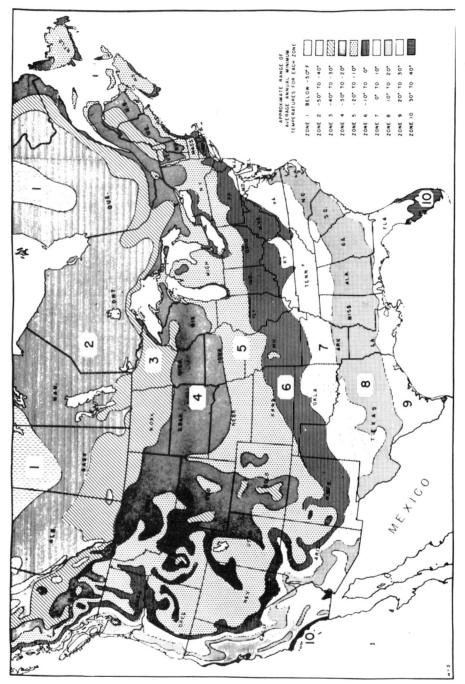

Plant hardiness zone map

1•Flowers to Enjoy in the Garden and in Bouquets

Fresh, fragrant flowers—what could be nicer? And whether your place in the sun or in the shade is a cramped ledge above a busy street or rambling acreage in the country, you can grow flowers. Don't worry if you weren't born with a green thumb. All you really need is to fit the right plant to the space you have, prepare the soil well before planting, and then use common sense in day-to-day care. Tender, loving care, that is.

No less than a pet cat or dog, a plant is a living, growing thing. In the absence of rain, it needs water. Unless your soil is uncommonly rich, it needs plant food. And if pest or disease should attack, you will have to do some plant doctoring. In the pages that follow you will find flowers for a whole season of bloom outdoors—from the first golden crocus that gets caught in a late winter snowstorm to the last chrysanthemum that defies Jack Frost. These are the plants to grow for color in the garden and plenty of cutting material for bouquets in the house. For shrubs with bright bloom and berries, see pages 71-4, for flowering trees see pages 60-2, for flowering vines see pages 81-3, and for house plants see pages 116-8 and 135.

Crocus and Other Little Bulbs Signal the End of Winter

Weeks before the "major" bulbs give their burst of bloom—hyacinths, daffodils, and tulips—the "minor" bulbs splash their welcome color over the cold, damp earth. All grow only a few inches tall, all grow from small bulbs you plant 2" or 3" deep outdoors in autumn. Besides crocus they include golden winter aconite, blue scilla or squill, snowflake, glory-of-the-snow, grape-hyacinth, hardy bulbous Iris reticulata and I. danfordiae, and snowdrops. After the blooms fade, you can forget them until the following spring. Just try not to dig into the bulbs when you plant summer flowers over them. And if you've planted them in a meadow, don't mow it low until the bulb leaves have ripened, which they show by turning yellow and then drying up.

Hyacinths. The big Dutch hybrid hyacinths look best in clumps of three or more, or in formal beds or rows at least three deep. Early fall is the ideal planting season. When the blooms begin to fade, snap them off before seeds begin to form, but leave the hyacinth foliage to store up next year's flowers. Remove after it turns yellow, but meanwhile you can help hide it by interplanting with flowering transplants of such annuals as petunias, verbenas, and phlox.

Daffodils/narcissus. The poet saw a "host of golden daffodils," but

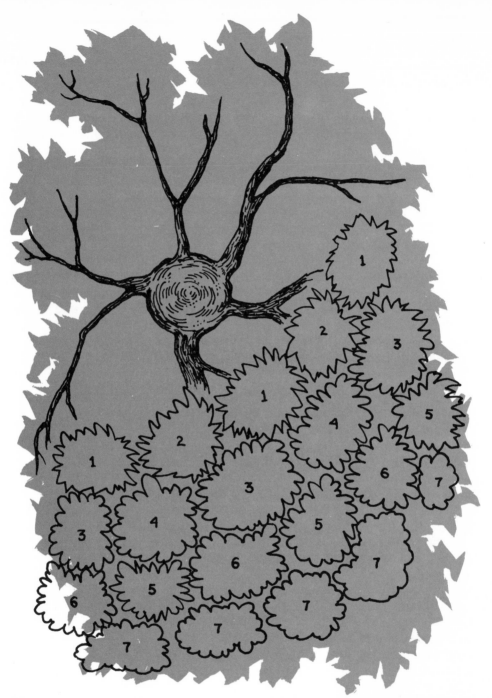

Shady garden with a tree cover. *1. Hardy maidenhair fern. 2. Hardy sword fern. 3. Hosta or plantain-lily. 4. Fancy-leaved caladium. 5. Forget-me-not. 6. Chionodoxa (glory-of-the-snow). 7. Spring pansy border, followed by impatiens for summer and fall bloom.*

that was a long time ago. Today he might see them in snowy white or luscious pink. Or frilled, doubled, bicolored, or big as a saucer. Daffodils are prettiest in the cultivated garden when planted in clumps of at least six of one variety, spaced 6" apart and about 6" deep. Early fall is the best time to plant, but any time up until the ground freezes hard is acceptable.

Daffodil hybrids and the charming species types usually referred to as "narcissus" are the best bulbs of all for naturalizing in a wild garden. In early fall, toss the bulbs over a grassy area. Plant each where it falls, 6" deep. The result? Spring flowers growing as naturally as if Mother Nature had planted them. If you allow the leaves to mature and turn yellow before mowing over the area, the bulbs will increase yearly, rewarding you with ever increasing numbers of flowers.

Tulips. Excepting sky blue, tulips have everything going for them in color, plus a long-run season that begins with certain species or "botanicals" which bloom at the end of winter, and ends with all kinds of May-flowering hybrids. Plant the bulbs about 5" deep and as much apart any time from early fall until the ground freezes. They're great for beds, borders, and planting pockets anywhere. Fosteriana, Greigii, and Kaufmanniana hybrids are superb in a rock garden (see page 121). About the only way tulips don't show off well is planted single file, marching up the front walk soldier fashion.

For best results, tulips need well-drained soil and full sun in the spring. Summer shade is fine while they're dormant, but the bulbs don't like soggy, wet soil. As soon as the flower petals fade, snap off the seed pods, a process most gardeners call "dead-heading." This channels all energies to forming next year's flowers. Unless you want formal beds of precision-spaced tulips, all in bloom at exactly the same time, the bulbs can be left in the ground permanently.

Lilies and other hardy bulbs. Hardy bulbs you plant once in the fall—and then forget except when they bloom—don't stop in May with the last tulip. Other kinds give flowers all season. Fairest of all are the true lilies, members of the genus Lilium. Best to plant are the hybrids, for example, vivid orange-red, tiger-spotted Enchantment. From the pristine Madonnas to the heavenly Rubrum and Auratum hybrids of late summer, there are hundreds of spectacular hardy lilies. Plant the bulbs in late fall or early spring, in moist, humus-rich, well-drained soil. In hot, dry climates, they'll do best in half shade; elsewhere, lilies need a half day or more of sunlight.

Alliums, otherwise known as ornamental onions, require the same culture as the hardy lilies. They aren't as well distributed commercially, but well worth searching out. Some grow less than 12" tall and bloom in the spring, others rise to 3' or more and may burst into all their glory at any time from then until August.

Pale pink lycoris, colchicums, fall-blooming crocus, and sternbergias represent another group of hardy bulbs—all with a surprising habit. They grow leaves in spring, abruptly die to the ground in early summer, only to return in August and September in the form of bouquets of leafless flowers. Best planting time is during the brief period of summer dormancy. Over-plant with low-growing ground cover such as alyssum, rose-moss, phlox, or verbena.

Tender bulbs. For sun, shade, and in-between there are tender bulbs that color the garden in a special way. "Tender" means that these can't survive freezing temperatures. And, while individual culture varies, the basic cycle is about the same: Tender bulbs are planted outdoors in the spring when the weather is settled and warm. They grow, flower, and store up strength for another season. When light frost nips the foliage the bulbs are dug, spaced out in shallow boxes, and placed to cure and dry in an airy, frost-free place.

Kinds with papery, onion-like skins, gladiolus for example, can be dried and cleaned, then hung in old nylon stockings until planting time. Bulbs more like a sweet potato—dahlia, tuberous begonia, and caladium, for example—or with fleshy roots attached to the bulb—Peruvian daffodil, for example—should be cleaned and stored in slightly moist peat moss or vermiculite. Check from time to time during winter to be sure the storage medium is moist, keeping the bulbs plump and firm. Of course, if digging, cleaning, and winter storage sound like too much trouble, you can simply treat tender bulbs like annual flowers; buy new stock every spring and let frost take them in the fall.

Considering that tuberous begonias are among the world's most beautiful flowers, they are not as difficult to grow as one might expect. Even in climates where summers are relentlessly hot and dry you can grow fairly decent tuberous begonias by situating them next to a north-facing wall where they can be kept moist and protected from hot, dry winds. In March, start the tubers indoors in a warm, moist, partly-sunny place. Transplant outdoors when the weather is settled. They can take direct sun early in the morning or in late afternoon, otherwise shade is needed. Plant in a mixture of garden loam, peat moss or leafmold, and sand. Keep moist at all times and apply fish-emulsion fertilizer every two weeks.

Fancy-leaved caladiums and the enormous green-leaved elephant-ear require the same care as tuberous begonias, although they thrive in tropical warmth. All are excellent for planting in semishady places, in beds, window boxes, pots, tubs, and other planters.

DeCaen or poppy-flowered anemones are what every non-gardener dreams of growing, but anyone who has ever tried knows not to believe the

Perennials beneath a small tree. *Use for added color before and after trees and shrubs have flowered. 1. Emerald Cushion euonymus or azalea. 2 Flowering dogwood or flowering crab apple. 3. Bunch-flowered tulips. 4. Daffodils. 5. Hyacinths. 6. Crocus and scilla, followed by impatiens and caladiums.*

glib catalog writer who says they are "easy to grow and thrive in any garden soil." They aren't and they won't.

But what a flower when you get an anemone to bloom! Actually, they need the kind of climate you might like to retire to—sunny days with moderate temperatures and pleasantly cool nights. If you'd like to give them a try, soak the dried-up-looking tubers in water of room temperature 24 hours prior to planting 2" deep and 4" apart in well-prepared soil. Culture for giant ranunculus or buttercups is the same. In mild-climate areas, anemones and ranunculus may be planted out in late fall for winter bloom; elsewhere, plant them out in the spring, the same as gladiolus.

There are dahlias with flowers smaller than a teacup and others larger than a dinner plate. There are 12" dwarfs and heroic varieties that could stand head to head with a basketball pro. They need rich, moist, well-drained soil in full sun. If you select a tall-growing variety, first firmly plant a sturdy stake of appropriate height. Then plant the tuber with its growth eye next to the stake. Position dahlia tubers 6" deep, but cover at first with only 2" of soil. As growth progresses, put in more soil, leaving a slight cavity to catch water. Use strips of soft plastic cut from garbage bags to keep the stems tied to the stake. Feed dahlias several times during the season and apply a thick mulch to conserve moisture.

Cannas need a long season of abundant moisture and warmth to really do their stuff. Plant the fleshy rhizomes about 2" deep after the weather is warm in the spring. In limited space, the Pfitzer Dwarfs are best; otherwise the Grand Opera Series hybrids. Calla-lilies, tuberoses, Peruvian daffodils, and the climbing lily (gloriosa, which is in no way related to the Gloriosa daisy) require care similar to that needed by the canna.

Of all the summer bulbs, gladiolus are the easiest to grow and the least expensive. They need well-drained, average garden soil and a place with at least half a day of direct sun. Plant 3" to 5" deep in clumps of at least 10 of one color or variety. For cut flowers only, plant glads in easy-to-cultivate rows in the vegetable garden. For longest bloom season, study catalogs of gladiolus specialists and order early, midseason, and late varieties, and make three plantings two weeks apart of each kind.

Other bulbs that grow as gladiolus include tigridia, freesia, sparaxis, ixia, Dutch iris, watsonia, summer hyacinth, and acidanthera, the fragrant gladiolus. In mild-winter climates, fall-planted freesias, Dutch irises, sparaxis, and ixias give winter and spring bloom.

Annuals for Great Bloom in a Single Season

Annuals are the quickest, easiest, and least expensive way to fill a whole garden with flowers. They have the remarkable ability of completing the life cycle—growing from seed to bloom and setting new seeds for their own perpetuation—within the few short weeks of summer. From the brilliant, flaming pink foliage of the Joseph's-coat amaranthus to the familiar "down home" zinnia there are annual flowers in every imaginable size, growth habit, and color.

Iceland poppies, perhaps the most ethereally beautiful of all, are typical of the hardy annuals—the "hardy" meaning you can sow the seeds outdoors in late fall or winter. They'll germinate in the first warm spell, and be ready to bloom by late spring. Larkspur and bachelor's-button or cornflower also belong in this category. Besides enjoying hardy annuals in the garden, you can broadcast their seeds over an open meadow or along the road. They will grow as if planted by nature and keep coming back every year from self-sown seeds.

If you have a piece of ground that is bare, hot, and dry in the summer, rose-moss or portulaca may be the answer. Broadcast the seeds where they are to grow. More will sprout if you moisten the area by misting with water after sowing, and then lightly mulch with a scant layer of straw. Rose-moss does best in sandy, lean soil. The newest and best kinds of rose-moss are F1 hybrids, a designation you'll find on seed packets of the best varieties of all annuals.

Marigolds are more than pretty—they scare away the bugs, at least according to most organic gardeners (see page 34). Given a spot with at least a half day of direct sun, nothing could be easier to grow than a marigold. Whether you start from seeds planted early in the house, or directly in the garden after the soil is warm, or from flats of seedlings purchased at your neighborhood garden center, marigolds are a sure thing. The dwarf French types, often used as edgers for the tall American hybrids, are ideal for sunny window boxes and patio containers. Cut marigolds by the armful for bouquets, or otherwise keep faded flowers cut. That's all you do to keep them blooming until hard freezing in autumn. Best of today's large-flowered varieties are F1 hybrids. If you dislike the odor of marigolds on your hands after working with them, rub table salt on your hands as you wash them with soap and water.

Given ideal conditions, almost all annual flowers are easy to grow from seeds, but certain kinds are best bought as started plants, at least in my experience. Among these I think first of petunias, one of today's finest annual flowers, but also of verbena, annual phlox (Phlox drummondii), flowering sage or salvia, and ageratum. The truth is, you can set out a garden of these nursery-grown seedlings in a matter of minutes, add a 2" mulch of bark chips, water well—and relax. You'll have put in an "instant" garden that will bloom all summer, yet require almost no attention from you other than admiration.

For beauty in cut flowers, no annual quite equals the China-aster or

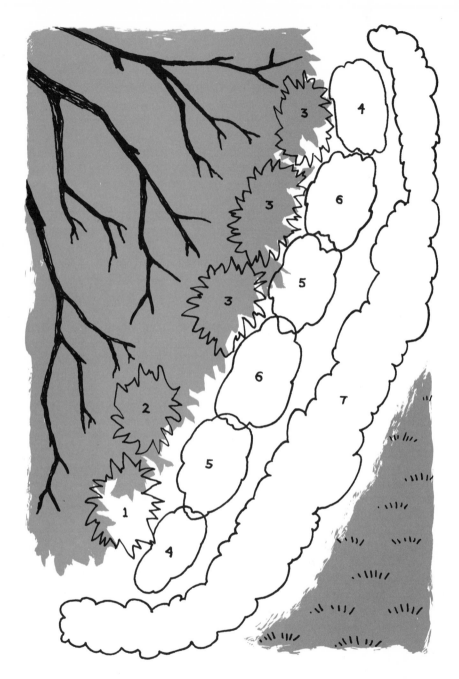

Flowers by a wooded path. *Small bulbs can be tucked anywhere there is a few inches of soil. 1. Lily-of-the-valley. 2. Forget-me-not. 3. Mertensia (Virginia bluebells). 4. Sweet violets. 5. Columbine. 6. Bleeding-heart. 7. Assorted hardy ferns.*

callistephus. If you buy these as started plants, accept only those seedlings with healthy, crisp, green foliage. Reject any with yellow or wilted lower leaves. Whether you grow China-asters from started plants or from seeds in your own garden, plant them in deeply-spaded, well-drained soil. Then mulch with bark chips or cocoa bean hulls and be sure they never wilt for lack of moisture. Given this care and at least four hours of direct sun daily, every plant will turn into a bouquet of bloom from mid-summer to early fall.

Some annual flowers are actually tender perennials. This means that in frost-free climates they may live on year after year, but in cold-winter areas they are treated as any other annual. Wax begonias and dusty miller, along with snapdragons, bedding geraniums, and impatiens are tender perennials. Started from seeds, all need three months or more in a sunny, moist, moderate temperature, fresh-air atmosphere to reach flowering size. Unless you're really into gardening, pick up transplants at your local garden center.

Breeders are making vast improvements in begonias and snap-dragons. Look for the F1 hybrid designation. Snapdragons are ideal cut flowers; the more you cut the more they'll bloom.

Wax begonias are for edging, bedding in masses of a single color, or monochromatically, for instance, light and dark pink with red, and for pots and window boxes. Unlike tuberous begonias, they have a fibrous root system and won't grow properly without a few hours of direct sun. (And, of course, wax begonias also make almost foolproof flowering house plants.)

Cockscomb and other everlastings represent the sort of endless summer feeling that annual flowers in general carry. First, they color the garden with fresh flowers, then you cut them while they are still in peak condition, tie the stems in loose bunches, and hang upside down to dry in an airy, shaded place. You can make beautiful arrangements of dried flowers to enjoy indoors all fall and winter. The vivid color of fresh cocks-comb dries to the subtle and royal red of a fine, old Oriental rug; the brilliant golds become richer, less brash.

Other annuals that dry well include strawflower, statice, globe amaranth, acroclinium or helipterum, pearl everlasting, immortelle, ammobium, and rhodanthe. They combine perfectly with dried ornamental grasses such as avena, coix, and lagurus.

So many annual flowers require a place in the sun it may seem that shady gardens have to be glades of ferns and other greenery. Not so. Impatiens and coleus are two annuals that bring rich, jewel colors to shaded areas. Start with young plants from your garden center in the spring. Favorite varieties can be wintered over from cuttings taken in the fall, rooted in a glass of water, then transplanted to pots of soil.

Flowering tobacco or nicotiana is another annual flower that does well in shade; not in a dark, gloomy place, but in pleasant, dappled light found under a tall shade tree, or in a window box on the north-facing side of a building. Although hybrid nicotiana is available in several colors—red, mauve, chartreuse—the white-flowered types are the most dependably fragrant, especially at night.

Perennials for Flowers in All Seasons

From the first dwarf iris that flirts its velvety petals with early spring snow-fall—to the greenish-white Christmas-rose (Helleborus niger, not a true rose) that really does bloom during warm spells in the middle of winter, there are sturdy perennial flowers. The ethereal beauty of flowers is not to be tallied up like a balance sheet, but hardy herbaceous perennials do yield a big return, year after year, on a very small investment.

"Herbaceous" means that the stems are not persistently woody. Every spring they sprout from roots that live through winter in ground that is often cold, wet, and solidly frozen. The common peony with its uncommonly beautiful flowers is a perfect example. Dormant peony roots planted 2" deep in late summer send up in the spring bronzy green foliage and sturdy stems topped by the fragrant flowers. Thereafter, the foliage remains handsome until freezing in autumn, when they once more take to the underground until warm weather returns.

But, like a truly great perennial, once planted in well-drained soil in a sunny place, where it doesn't have to compete with greedy tree or shrub roots, the peony needs no particular attention, and hardly ever needs to be dug and divided. The so-called tree peonies are true woody plants, and, as such, are considered shrubs (see page 72).

Basket-of-gold alyssum, known officially as Aurinia saxatilis, is like a swatch of warm spring sunshine captured in a mat of flowers. It's a perfect choice for any kind of rock garden in the sun, but especially when planted so it can cascade over the top of a wall or rock outcropping. The variety citrinum is worth looking for because of its coloring that is more refined than the usual variety.

Trilliums, often called "wake robin," open three-petaled flowers of purest white, or sometimes purple, in early spring. These are the perfect choice for planting in a partly-shaded, nearly-wild garden. Give them moist, well-drained soil enriched with a lot of partly rotted leaves from a woodland—or your own compost pile. Like all American native wild flowers, unless they grow in abundance on your own property, it's best to buy started trillium plants from a nursery that specializes in wildlings.

Flowers for a shady north entrance. *At the north foundation of the house there is often room for a small perennial bed. Such places usually receive an hour or two of filtered sun from east or west during midsummer. There are a number of perennials suitable for such a planting spot. 1. Gaiety euonymus. 2. Lilliputian magnolia. 3. Assorted hardy fern. 4. Giant elephant's-ear. 5. Lily-of-the-valley. 6. Royal Robe violet. 7. Mertensia (Virginia bluebells). 8. Tuberous begonias. 9. Caladiums. 10. Impatiens. 11. Fernleaf bleeding-heart.*

Polyanthus hybrid primroses are typical of many early-spring flowers; they need sun at the beginning of the season—which gives them the necessary warmth for springing into precocious bloom. As the season advances, however, they appreciate some cooling shade. Set out started plants in spring or fall. They are ideal companions for tulips and daffodils.

The exquisite lily-of-the-valley is one of the toughest of the hardy perennials. Use it as a ground cover in a partly-sunny to fully-shaded spot. For a quick cover, plant the roots 12'' apart over the area. When the stems have grown into a crowded, thick mass, dig up immediately after spring flowering, pull or cut apart, and replant, having first enriched the soil with a generous sprinkling of fertilizer.

In May, tall bearded hybrid iris are the stars of many backyard gardens. Summer brings the fresh, heat-defying flowers of daylilies, which will grow from fountains of corn-like or grass-like foliage.

Shasta daisies (usually white-flowered) and painted daisies or pyrethrum (in vivid pinks) are actually fancy hybrids of the chrysanthemum. Set out young plants in the spring. They'll bloom in a few weeks and, like many annual flowers, the more you cut for bouquets, the more they'll bloom all summer.

The delicate-appearing bleeding-heart is actually a hardy perennial that grows easily in moist, well-drained soil in sun or shade. However, don't expect it to prosper in a parched, dry place.

Blanket flower or gaillardia is almost as tough as the daylily. When you buy seeds or plants, read the description carefully. Some are annual flowers, others perennial. Give it a place in the sun in well-drained, average—meaning not terribly rich—soil.

Hosta, also called funkia and plantain-lily, is cultivated first for handsome foliage, often variegated, but also for fragrant flowers. It thrives in partial shade in moist, humus-rich soil.

The elegant Japanese iris bloom in the summer—as late as August in some areas. They need lots of moisture, especially until flowering time. If you have a small stream or pond, plant Japanese iris along the banks, but not with the roots actually in a swamp-like bog.

Summer phlox put on a spectacular show in July and August, but they are among the perennials that need digging, dividing, and replanting every other year or two. Powdery mildew also disfigures the foliage, but it can be controlled by spraying with a fungicide. Once you see today's hybrids, you'll know the flower crop is worth a little trouble. But the dull magenta kinds that have gone nearly wild in old gardens probably aren't worth having in yours.

Five perennials for late summer flowers. Fragrant-leaved beebalm grows wild in sunny, moist places, but usually with flowers such a dirty lavender they go unnoticed. But what about the vivid red hybrid that is available from many nurseries? Or the bright, true pink? As a bonus, the foliage has a wonderful mint scent.

Liatris or Kansas gayfeather is an American native wild flower, often seen on dry roadsides in the Great Plains states. There are now varieties with just as much stamina to plant in your garden. Colors vary from lavender to a fairly dark purple, also pure white. They are great for cutting.

Echinops or globe-thistle has perfectly rounded globes of silvery-blue flowers. It grows tall and looks especially pretty in the company of late-blooming yellow daylilies.

Goldenglow is an American pioneer flower that survives even around farmhouses abandoned for a generation or more. Yet it is not an invasive weed. It grows to 8' tall and spreads out several feet as well. In other words, it needs space, but has few equals for brightening up the corner of an outbuilding on a large property.

Helenium, in improved varieties like Butter Pat, gives a thigh-high and fairly neat mound of flowers from late July until September. It needs sun and well-drained soil, otherwise it grows like a well-behaved weed.

Flowers for Autumn

Chrysanthemums are the glory of fall gardens, but don't overlook the hardy asters, available in sizes from 8'' dwarfs to bushes 5' tall. If frost comes early in your area, choose early-flowering chrysanthemum hybrids—the kinds bred at the University of Minnesota or at the North Platte Experiment Station in Nebraska (nursery catalogs list these kinds).

Chrysanthemums, unlike hardy asters and most other perennials, need to be divided every spring for best results. Replant only the strongest of the offshoots and discard the old, woody center of the plant. The football and spider types reach perfection only when carefully staked, tied, and disbudded, but there are countless garden types that will give a spectacular show. Mass them in gardens or grow only a few in pots.

All the World Loves a Rose

Of all the flowering plants from which to choose, hardly any equals the rose, especially today's best varieties which tend to be generally hardy, disease resistant, and fragrant. Books have been written about the culture of roses, which in fact is very simple—unless, of course, you want to join the American Rose Society and grow prize-winning blooms.

Roses need a site where they will receive a half-day or more of direct sunlight in well-drained, moist soil. Buy the best quality bushes you can find, either by mail from a rose specialist or locally from a garden center or nursery. Bargain rosebushes sold sometimes at $2 each or less are rarely worth the investment, let alone the effort it takes to plant them.

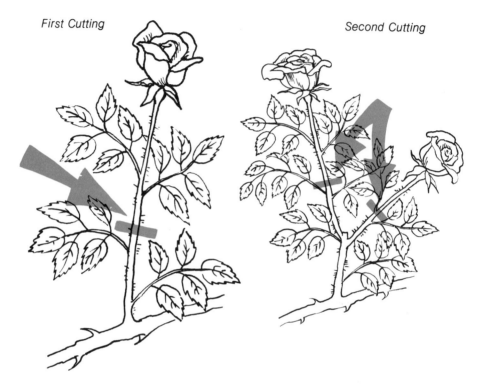

First Cutting

Second Cutting

Leave no more than two groups of leaves below the cut on the branch.

If you want your roses to be bug free, it will probably be necessary to spray or dust them periodically. There are products on the market which allow you to fertilize and apply pest and disease controls at the same time —all as granules applied to the soil. These work as systemics, through the root system of the rosebush.

Succulents for the Beauty of the Desert

Whether you live in a warm climate or in the cold North, there are cacti and other succulents that will live in your garden, making possible the

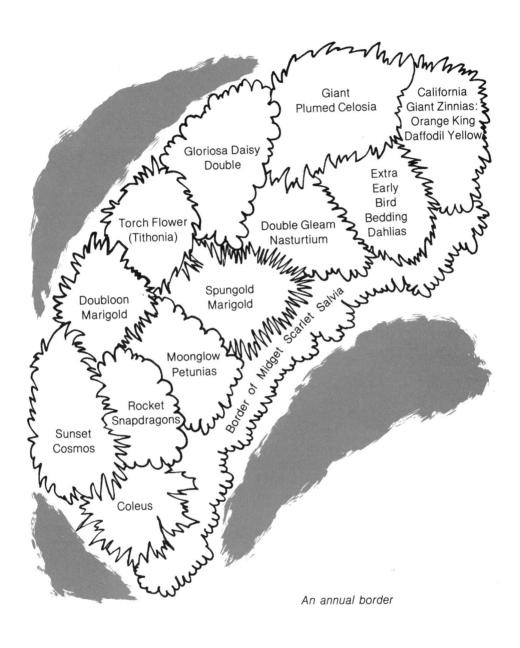

Giant
Plumed Celosia

California
Giant Zinnias:
Orange King
Daffodil Yellow

Gloriosa Daisy
Double

Extra
Early
Bird
Bedding
Dahlias

Torch Flower
(Tithonia)

Double Gleam
Nasturtium

Doubloon
Marigold

Spungold
Marigold

Border of Midget Scarlet Salvia

Moonglow
Petunias

Rocket
Snapdragons

Sunset
Cosmos

Coleus

An annual border

rare beauty of the desert—far from any windswept sand dune. In warm climates, some succulents often seen in gardens include aloe, agave, aeonium, crassula, echeveria, and kalanchoe. In cold climates, the hardy succulents include sempervivums, sedums, yuccas, and certain cacti found among the opuntia (prickly pear) and mammillaria types.

Container Gardens for Gardens Where You Want Them

There have been container gardens since Biblical times, but the idea has been vastly sophisticated by contemporary gardeners. The ideal plan today is to have a neatly-organized, convenient growing area, almost like having your own nursery, where you bring along container plants. Just as they burst into bloom you move them to an arrangement of great beauty at your front door, or around your outdoor living area—for example, blue ageratum, pink geraniums, and yellow daisies; or hybrid lilies in pots and pink geraniums alongside. When the flowers fade, the growing containers go back to the nursery area and something newly in bloom goes on stage. If you don't have the space, time, or the inclination for this approach, then you can make a studied grouping of container plants that come in and out of bloom, not all at the same time. Or you can concentrate kinds that bloom all in one season.

Just remember that containers dry out with amazing speed in hot weather. Daily watering is sometimes required, and feeding with a liquid fertilizer mixed according to container directions will be needed every two days to two weeks throughout the growing season.

Europeans and Pacific Northwest Canadians have always done fabulous things with window boxes—admittedly in climates gentler than we enjoy in most of the continental United States. Now we can create the same effect with today's super F1 hybrid impatiens, cascade-type petunias, and semperflorens or everblooming begonias, as well as geraniums, fuchsias, and caladiums. Set out young, vigorous seedlings in bud or bloom when the weather has settled in the spring. Keep the soil constantly moist and feed every 10 days to two weeks. The boxes will look like lush flower gardens until frost.

2•Trees for Shade, Flowers, and Other Benefits

Ornamental trees are a lifetime investment that beautifies your home and adds to its value. There is no sounder investment than trees carefully selected, correctly planted, and well cared for. They yield annual dividends in cooling shade and colorful flowers, and give homes that lived-in, planted look. Because they will grow into the most prominent features of your landscape, trees must be selected with care. Weigh the potential shapes and sizes. Base your selections on tree species that grow well in the local soil and climate and you won't need a green thumb to help your investment flourish. Wherever you live and under whatever conditions you must garden, there are beautiful trees of every sort—shade, flowering, evergreen—suited to your needs.

How to Tell the Trees from the Forest

Ornamental trees generally fall into three categories:

1. Shade trees with cool, green, summer foliage such as Norway maple, pin oak, linden, ash, or hybrid elm.
2. Flowering trees for a breathtaking blossom time, such as the purely ornamental flowering fruit trees, the saucer magnolia, and redbud.
3. Trees whose foliage is colorful, such as the Harlequin maple and the Crimson King maple.

Combined with some of the needled and the broadleaved evergreens, plantings that include some of each of these types present colorful patterns in every season. If you are a homeowner just starting out, shade trees will be your basic planting, the primary reason being cool, green, summer foliage. Next, add variety with some of the foliage trees. Then fill gaps with the smaller spring- and summer-flowering types.

Selecting Trees Primarily for Shade

There are about five basic shapes among the most-planted shade trees—the pyramid, the weeper, the vase, the globe, and the column. Some of each grow in every size you could need. A combination of these shapes and sizes adds interest to the landscape as long as the trees are in scale with the house and grounds, and as long as you don't plant too many. Remember, as you select, the ultimate height of the tree and the amount of shade it may cast on windows, lawn, and shrubbery.

Weeper. These are somewhat shaggy, enormously graceful trees with an informal look. They require space to show off their lines—and also because they tend to grow to be as wide as they are tall. Select smaller types—there are several flowering types—for small, city lots. The low-hanging branches of weepers create good screening.

Weeping trees include beech species, several crab apples, flowering cherry, the cutleaf weeping birch, the European ash, silver-pendant linden, Swedish cutleaf birch, and many types of willow.

Pyramid. The pyramids are trim and tidy shapes, excellent for lawn or street planting. They should be planted far enough apart to show off their outlines to best advantage and to allow sun to get beneath the branches to the grass and plantings below. The taller varieties in this shape shouldn't be planted right in front of the house—they are too big.

Pyramidal trees include Anise magnolia, European beech, ginkgo, littleleaf linden, plane tree, pin oak, red horse-chestnut, red maple, and whitebeam mountain-ash.

Column. These soaring, stately trees are the type used to create alleys on large estates. In the smaller landscape, they make handsome accents in the foreground of tree clumps, are useful along narrow side yards, and should be considered when screening is required.

The best-known columnar trees are the Bolleana poplars, but there are others: fastigiate goldenrain, the columnar ginkgo, the Japanese cherry, mountain-ash species, Norway maple, Sargent cherry, and the white birch.

Vase. The vase-shaped trees tend to produce more shade than the other types because of the high spreading branches. They are often large and require lots of space all around. Since grass may not succeed beneath them, plan to install a fast-spreading ground cover that succeeds in shady places (see page 91).

The Amur cork-tree tends to be vase-shaped as do the hackberry, Moraine locust, red oak, sugar maple, sweet gum, sycamore, the tulip tree, white ash, white oak, and zelkova.

Globe. These are sometimes round, sometimes oval and, because of their symmetry, give a formal look to the landscape. Because many are low-growing enough to mature without touching utility wires, they are often used in street planting. They also make lovely front yard lawn specimens.

Among the best globe-shaped trees are the Arnold crab apple, blue ash, globe locust, Japanese maple, Kwanzan cherry, Norway maple, and red maple.

How Tall Does a Tree Grow in Ten Years?

Trees grow at different rates, depending on the species itself, on the climate, soil, air, rainfall, and many other variables. As you plan, take into account the mature height of the tree as specified in a catalog or on a nursery tag. Then take into account the amount of light, which has a direct effect on the growth of every tree. Trees crowded together in close-planted stands reach for the light—and grow taller. Single specimens planted in a lawn grow wider but may not try to reach the sky quite as quickly. In soils that are rich in humus, well-drained, and well-supplied with nutrients, trees grow more rapidly than when planted in poor, dry, compacted soils.

In the North, because of the shortness of the growing season and because of light conditions, trees tend to grow more slowly. Trees exposed to constant winds, as they are at the seashore in many areas, may always remain dwarfed. Trees growing in difficult city conditions may also reach their maturity slowly. Like children, trees grow more quickly in their early years than in their later years. Young Norway spruces have recorded annual growth gains of 40", but the more mature Norway spruce may grow 18" or less in a good year. At full maturity, tree growth slows to just a few inches annually.

Ornamental Trees for Summer Shade and Beauty

Trees rarely fail if they are suited to the region or location you have selected as their home. One way to be sure the tree you want to grow belongs in your backyard is to stick to locally-grown nursery stock. Almost every type (genus) of tree has species or varieties suited to the special climate conditions of its general region, and the local garden center usually knows which is which. Here are some of the best.

Pin oak (Quercus palustris) grows to about 40' and succeeds in USDA Hardiness Zone 5 (see the map on page 38) and southward. A medium oak of symmetrical shape, it is native to the moist eastern lowlands—"palustris" means swamp. The common name "pin oak" refers to the many slender, drooping branches, some of which may sweep the forest floor in its native habitat. Good for street and lawn planting, but needs plenty of room. It is slow to leaf out in spring, but the dark crimson foliage lasts into late autumn.

Tuliptree Ginkgo White Spruce   Catalpa Black Larch Sugar Maple

Red Maple Paper Birch Yellowwood   Red Mulberry   White Oak

Willow Oak   Horsechestnut   Chestnut Oak   Sweetgum

American Birch American Linden   Black Oak   Shellback Hickory

Sequoia Scarlet Oak Red Cedar   Mimosa Hackberry Redwood

Size of mature shade trees in relation to the height of a 2-story house. Each horizontal line represents 10 feet.

Norway maple (Acer platanoides) grows to about 35' and succeeds North through Zone 4. About the best all-around shade tree, it grows well in gardens or along city streets. Its dense foliage is a dark, rich green. It turns yellow in fall. Leaves remain from early spring to late fall. A hardwood maple, it withstands wind and ice breakage.

Norway maple (variety Emerald Queen) grows to 30' or 35' and is good in Zone 4 and southward. It grows more quickly than the previously-mentioned species, has darker foliage, and is better adapted to withstand hot Midwestern sun and wind. Both these trees are rounded in shape and suited for shading low, sprawling, ranch-type homes.

Russian mulberry (Morus tatarica) grows to about 25' and succeeds north through Zone 5. This is a fast-growing shade tree for lawns and well suited for use in windbreaks as it spreads to about 25' in width. Mulberries can be used for jams and jellies and to attract birds. Planted near cherry trees, the mulberry acts as a decoy to cherry-hungry birds.

Moraine ash (Fraxinus variety) grows to about 40' and succeeds in Zone 5 and southward. A member of the olive family, it is a lovely tree for backyard and street planting. Medium in size, it has a round head and brilliant green foliage that turns yellow-purple in fall.

Little-leaf linden (Tilia cordata) grows to a height of 50' and succeeds north through Zone 4. A rounded, compact tree, it prefers rich, but not wet, soil. The heart-shaped leaves are dense. The tree grows quickly and its fragrant cream-colored blossom clusters attract a great many bees. If soil grows too dry in hot weather, leaves may fall.

Green King hybrid elm (Ulmus variety) grows only to a height of 50' but it is resistant to the diseases that have taken such a heavy toll of the other elms. Successful in most of the country, Zones 10 through 3, it is one of the fastest growing shade trees and has straight, sturdy branches and dark-green foliage. It is extra hardy and is being recommended for park, lawn, and street planting from Florida to Canada.

Redmond linden (Tilia variety) reaches a height of 40' and succeeds in Zone 4 and southward. One of the finest shade trees, it transplants easily, grows vigorously, and resists the troublesome winter trio of wind, ice, and snow. The dark-green leaves are large and in winter the bare crimson-tipped branches are highly decorative.

Cutleaf weeping birch (Betula variety) grows to about 65' and succeeds to Zone 2. A variety of the lovely European birch, the branches weep strongly, making it an interesting specimen for prominent positions. It is more affected by drought than the other members of the clan and shows stress if not watered during very dry, hot weather.

Black walnut (Juglans nigra) is a spectacular tree that grows to 150' in the eastern United States though it stays below 100' in height in the

West. Its crown is round with furrowed, flaking brown bark. The nuts are small, hard to shell but very good. It has a reputation for inhibiting growth in gardens nearby and usually is planted in the open. Succeeds to Zone 5.

Horse-chestnut (Aesculus species and varieties) grows to about 60' and succeeds through Zone 2. A pyramidal tree that casts extremely dense shade, it has ornamental flowers in spring that are red in the species A. carnea, a smaller tree better suited to small landscapes.

Cottonless cottonwood (Populus deltonides) reaches a height of 75' or more and succeeds to Zone 4. It has all the qualities of the cottonwood, a fast growing, tough tree with low maintenance. Since it is grown from cuttings that do not bear seed, there is no cotton to cloud pond surfaces and catch in shrubbery and one's hair. This is an excellent shade tree, also recommended for windbreaks.

Flowering Trees for Spring Beauty

There are trees both tall and small that fill the sky with blossoms and fragrance come spring, and no modern landscape is complete without them. Among the best are the flowering fruit trees, but there are many others, suited to the range of climates across the United States.

Pygmy saucer magnolia (Magnolia soulangeana Lilliputian) is a charming little tree that grows 8' to 10' tall and is suited to the flower border or shrubbery bed. It succeeds through Zone 5. More prolific than many of the larger forms, it has magnificent flowers, white inside, purple outside, that bloom in the very early spring. Plant in a sheltered place with fairly moist, porous soil, preferably sandy or peaty loam. Above mid-Iowa it may need some shelter from wind in open locations.

Tree wisteria (Wisteria floribunda) is another small tree for Zones 9 through 5. Covered with weeping blossoms in spring, it is best in formal gardens or as a featured specimen. The umbrella shape is achieved by light pruning. It needs deep, rich loam on the moist side and should be fertilized after leaves have fallen. Avoid spring or summer feeding and plant in full sun. It is not recommended for planting in the Canadian border states from Maine to Idaho, and it doesn't stand up to weather in most sections of northern Wisconsin.

Redbud, Judas tree (Cercis canadensis) grows to about 20' and flourishes through Zone 5. A companion to the dogwood, it covers itself with rose-colored flowers before the heart-shaped leaves unfurl. In a limited space, it offers some shade and is effective planted behind low-growing shrubbery. Transplant the redbuds while small as the larger trees resent moving. The redbud requires well-drained soil. The name "Judas tree'' recalls the legend that the flowers blush because Judas Iscariot is said to have hanged himself on a tree of this type.

Flowering dogwood (Cornus florida) grows to a height of 15' to 25' and flourishes through Zone 5. Leave a space of 20' between dogwoods because the layered branches spread widely. Dogwoods grow in average soil and are adapted to sun or light shade. This tree is shallow rooted, so avoid planting anything but grass beneath it. The tiered branches studded with turreted buds become a cloud of creamy white in spring when the four-petaled bracts surrounding the tiny true flowers open. Foliage turns to wine-red at summer's end and is flecked with red berries the robins enjoy.

Pink-flowering dogwood (Cornus rubra) grows to the same height and succeeds in the same climates as the white dogwood. Cherokee Chief is a variety with blossoms close to true red. It grows to about 12'. The new leaves are a brilliant green that turn scarlet in the fall.

Flowering peach (Prunus variety) grows to about 15' and succeeds through Zone 6. Number one on the spring color parade, the huge double blossoms of varieties such as Double Scarlet, Snowbank, Pink Charmer, and Peppermint Stick make the tree everything a flowering tree can be. The flowering peaches succeed in the same climate and soil conditions as the trees grown for fruit.

Flowering crab apple (Malus variety) comes in sizes ranging from 8' to 20', depending on the variety, and succeeds through Zone 4. White to crimson in color range, flowering crab apples also produce small, colorful fruit in fall. Some varieties have silver-gray or bronze-red foliage. The lovely spring-flowering trees are used as lawn specimens, for screening, and for limited shade. Soil and growing conditions are the same as for ordinary fruiting apple trees.

Flowering Trees for Summer Beauty

Tree hydrangea (Hydrangea arborescens) grows to about 10' and succeeds through Zone 4. Plant this handsome little tree wherever late summer color is needed, along the drive or at the lawn's edge. Adapted to varying conditions, it performs best in rich, moist soil. Mammoth blossom clusters change from creamy white to pink in the fall. Cut back all new growth to two buds in the fall or early spring.

Japanese stewartia (Stewartia pseudo-camellia) grows to 30' tall and succeeds through Zone 7. The flowers resemble single white camellias and appear in July and August. The foliage turns from bronze to dark purple in the fall. The stewartias are all-season performers that exhibit interesting branch patterns in winter, pretty pointed leaves in spring, and stage their flower and foliage displays in summer and fall. Slow growing, they are best in moist, acid soil and will burn when young unless well watered.

Franklinia altamaha (the Benjamin Franklin tree) grows 20' to 30' tall and flourishes through Zone 6. The flowers, white with a center cluster of yellow stamens, open from round white buds in August and September and sometimes are in bloom when the foliage begins to turn. Best in well-drained, rich, slightly acid soil, it needs partial shade in hot summer regions. It is handsome used in contrast to rhododendrons.

Waterer laburnum (Laburnum watereri), a cross between Scotch laburnum and the common goldenchain tree, grows to about 30' and succeeds through Zone 5. Hanging clusters of yellow, pea-shaped flowers droop much like wisteria and bloom in late spring to early summer, depending on the region. Well-drained, somewhat acid soil, and protection from hot afternoon sun in warmer regions are its main requirements.

Trees With Colorful Foliage

When we speak of color in foliage, we tend to think of autumn color, and no one will deny its importance or beauty in the landscape at the end of the year. However, there are trees that are colorful all year long. When you are planning for autumn color, plan, too, for color that begins in spring and stays through the summer.

Sunburst locust (Robinia variety) reaches a height of 25' and flourishes through Zone 4. Like a bouquet of sunshine, the graceful, green, fern-like branches are tipped with golden leaves all summer. Adapted to variable soils, it will grow almost anywhere, even in city air pollution. Lovely as a lawn specimen. This sturdy little tree weathers ice storms well, and is seedless, so there are no messy pods to litter.

Purple-leaf plum (Prunus Newport) reaches a height of 15' or so, succeeds through Zone 4, and is hardy. It sometimes is grown as a shrub, kept small by pruning. The pink blossoms are often mistaken for those of the flowering cherry. In fact, the purple-leaf plum is grown instead of the flowering cherry in cold winter sections. Suited to a variety of soils within its hardiness zone, it is treated as other plum trees.

Crimson King maple (Acer platanoides schwedleri nigra) reaches a height of 35' and grows everywhere through Zone 4. It is the showiest of all the fall foliage trees and succeeds in soils suited to the other maples.

Harlequin variegated-leaf maple (Acer platanoides aureomarginatum) grows to about 30' and succeeds through Zone 4. A Norway maple, this unusual tree has frosty, white-edged leaves. A globe-shaped specimen, it responds to the conditions suited to other Norway maples. Occasionally one branch will bear leaves that are all green; cut out such a branch.

Sugar maple (Acer saccharum) reaches 50' and flourishes through Zone 4 and even farther north. Brilliant in its red and gold October garb, this is one of the loveliest of the native hardwoods. The sugar maple requires spreading room. Don't expect to grow just any of the ground covers in its deep shade; try ferns, pachysandra, or trailing myrtle (Vinca minor). Well-drained uplands are the sugar maple's natural habitat and in this setting it grows rapidly.

Schwedler Norway maple (Acer platanoides schwedleri) is a handsome tree 50' to 60' tall that succeeds through Zone 4. It has striking, purplish-red leaves in spring which later turn to dark, bronzy green, and then become golden in fall. A broad-crowned tree, it is adaptable to many soils and conditions, but performs poorly in alkaline soils.

Rubylace locust (Gleditsia triachanthos), a cousin of the Sunburst locust, has foliage that shades to bright ruby-red. The color lasts from spring through August. A hardy tree through Zone 4, it grows to about 20' in most situations.

Tulip tree (Liriodendron species) is a majestic tree native to the Eastern states that reaches to 80' in height and succeeds through Zone 5. Sometimes 40' across, it has a straight trunk with spreading, rising branches that form a tall, pyramidal crown. The tulip-shaped flowers appear in late spring and are greenish-yellow, orange at the base, and handsome close up. Fall foliage is a lovely yellow. This tree requires lots of room, a deep, rich, well-drained neutral to slightly acid soil, and plenty of water in summer.

Russian olive (Elaeagnus species) grows to be 20' to 30' tall and is hardy as far north as Zone 4. Its great beauty is its silvery foliage and shaggy, dark-brown bark. Small, greenish-yellow flowers in early summer are fragrant. This tree can take almost any amount of heat and wind in the interior but does poorly and is out of place in mild-winter, cool-summer climates.

Red cutleaf maple (Acer palmatum) is the lovely little red Japanese maple whose brilliant foliage in spring and fall makes it one of the most attractive of all small trees. Slow growing to 20', this variety has deeply-lobed leaves and branches that are bright green. Leaves generally hold the red tones all summer. Give some shelter from hot sun. Successful through Zone 5.

Cornus Rainbow (Cornus florida welchii) is rainbow dogwood, a recent introduction. This medium-size tree has variegated leaves whose color changes as the season progresses, from yellow and green through spring and summer to scarlet, blue-lavender, and then greenish-purple in the fall. The flowers are less flamboyant than those of other flowering dogwoods. Hardy through Zone 5.

Selected Trees for Special Places

Whatever your needs and whatever your soil or climate, there are trees that fit the bill. Wet soil, dry soil, hill or valley, there are handsome specimens that will grow. If you don't easily find what you are looking for at the local nursery, keep checking the catalogs—sooner or later you will run across a tree that suits the situation and is just what you want.

Wet land appeals to several types of trees. The pink French pussy willow (Salix discolor caprea) is a petite tree, about 15' tall with giant, furry catkins that is tolerant of very damp soil and can be naturalized by a pond or stream. The catkins turn from gray to silver pink to rose as the weather warms. Succeeds through Zone 3.

Fast-growing weeping willow (Salix alba tristis) reaches 40' and tolerates moist soils or ordinary soils. Plant a small branch in moist soil in early spring and it will root and grow several feet by fall; in four years it will look like a mature tree. Loveliest weeping over a pond or stream, the willows also make handsome lawn specimens. This variety has lovely yellow-green catkins in the beginning of spring. Hardy through Zone 3.

Easy-to-spot white-barked birches are often planted where their chalky trunks can outline curved drives at night. The white birch (Betula pendula) reaches a height of 30' and has graceful branches in whose light shade grass can grow. Hardier than the white birch is the paper-white birch (Betula papyrifera) which grows to 35' and is able to withstand the winters of Zone 2. The bark, coated with a powdery white substance, peels in shaggy strips revealing a cream-colored inner bark. The leaves turn golden in autumn.

Sun is necessary to the cutleaf weeping birch (Betula pendula variety), the loveliest of all the birches. White-barked with weeping, willow-like branches, the finely-cut leaves are a lovely spring-pale shade of green. Succeeds through Zone 2.

Dry conditions are no hindrance to the mountain-ash (Sorbus aucuparia) and it isn't particular as to soil. Rapid growing, it succeeds through Zone 4 and southward. Graceful, green, fern-like leaves, light smooth bark, and creamy-white blossom sprays, followed by red berries in late summer, make it a highly desirable specimen.

Tough city conditions present no problems to the lovely and sturdy Ginkgo biloba, the maidenhair tree. Successful as far north as Zone 5, the ginkgo has leathery, light-green leaves until autumn, when they become gold. Mature trees are generally up to 40' tall, but under some conditions the ginkgo reaches 70' to 80'. Plant only male trees, as the females produce messy, bad-smelling fruits. Plant in deep, loose, well-drained soil. Stake young trees to keep them straight. A remarkably disease- and insect-free tree.

Trees for Windbreaks and Screening

Windbreaks are vital to the open plains country and increasingly so to urbanized areas where the noise and movement of fast traffic is a year-round problem. A well-planned tree and shrub barrier can eliminate noise just as a 35' windbreak of living trees can reduce a 30-mile-per-hour wind to 10 miles within 100' of the leeward side. Among trees successfully used as windbreaks are the pyramidal Bolleana poplar, the Russian olive, the cottonless cottonwood, Norway spruce, Jack pine, Ponderosa pine, Black Hills spruce, and Austrian pine. Some others appear in the text which follows.

Canaert red cedar (Juniperus virginiana variety) grows to about 40' and is one of the most popular of the tree junipers. It grows slowly but succeeds in poor soil and withstands strong winds. To avoid cedar-apple rust, don't plant with apple or crab apple trees.

Giant arbor-vitae (Thuja plicata) has an open growth with leaf sprays that are bright green with yellowish ends. Neat and symmetrical in its growth, it reaches to 60' tall in cultivation. Needs moisture to look its best.

Eastern white pine (Pinus strobus) is native from Newfoundland to Manitoba, south to Georgia, and as far west as Illinois and Iowa. Slow in the seedling stage, it grows quickly as it matures and reaches 100' or more. Hardy in any cold, it needs regular supplies of water. A symmetrical tree with blue-green needles.

Lombardy poplar (Populus nigra italica) reaches to 50' and succeeds as far north as Zone 2. A stately, fast-growing tree, the branches grow straight up and give the tree a tapering, cylindrical shape. Grows readily in any soil and very rapidly even through dry hot summer. Plant young trees 6' to 8' apart. Does not have a long life.

Chinese elm (Ulmus pumila) grows to 50' tall and succeeds through Zone 4. This is an excellent tree to use as a windbreak and it will flourish on poor alkaline soil and survive extremes in cold and drought. Good for tall or low hedging, it grows very quickly and supplies almost instant shade for homes and livestock. Plant young trees 4' to 6' apart.

Moreheim Colorado spruce (Picea pungens variety) grows to 100' tall, particularly in its native region, the West. An excellent tree for screening when young, it begins to lose its lower branches after about 20 years. Plant low-growing evergreens to the leeward side to compensate for later loss of its lower branches. Hardy through Zone 2.

The Needled Evergreen Trees

No landscape is complete without a scattering of needled evergreens. These majestic trees with their graceful foliage green the view when the deciduous trees have lost their foliage. Long-lived, they have relatively few problems and generally survive in soils of almost any composition as long as it is well drained and not overly alkaline. The spruces and the pines are among the most impressive. Within each genus, there is an extraordinary range of shapes and sizes. Many are native to North America and most are quite hardy.

Pinon pine (Pinus edulis) is native to the American Southwest. A slow-growing tree that stops between 10' and 20', the branches grow horizontally. A beautiful, small pine for containers, rock gardens, and shrub borders. The cones contain edible nuts and the wood, when burned, gives a marvelous fragrance.

Aleppo pine (Pinus halepensis) is native to the Mediterranean region and grows fairly quickly to between 30' and 60'. An attractive young tree, when mature it is nearly columnar with an irregular open crown. It thrives in desert heat, drought, wind, and is good at the seashore. Semihardy and very useful in poor soils and arid climates.

Japanese black pine (Pinus thunbergiana) grows quickly to 100' or more. Hardy, it is widely planted throughout California, western Washington, and Oregon in intermediate and high desert country. Accepts pruning readily as a young tree and is much used for bonsai training.

Monterey pine (Pinus radiata) is another native of the central West Coast. A quick-growing tree, it reaches 80' to 100' and can be pruned to maintain its denseness. This is not indicated for planting in desert areas nor in climates where temperatures go below 15°F in winter.

Evergreen Trees of Other Types

Handsome evergreens that are not needled grow in every climate. Some of the most beautiful broadleaved evergreens grow in climates where the temperatures stay above 25° or 30°F; some species of other types of trees are evergreen in warmer areas, not in cold ones—the ficus or fig, for instance. Evergreens that look more like broadleaved evergreens than needled evergreens—for instance, arbor-vitae—grow everywhere in one species or another. Nurseries make many evergreen species available in each climatic zone. Choose the type that appeals most to you, then investigate the shapes and sizes of the many varieties in each group before making a decision on which suits your landscape best. In colder regions, some of the loveliest flowering shrubs are broadleaved evergreens and grow to tree size (see pages 73-4).

Eucalyptus, a genus imported from its native Australia, grows well in California and other regions where temperatures stay above 25° or 30°F in winter. The dwarf blue gum (Eucalyptus globulus compacta) is a handsome, low-growing specimen that survives temperatures slightly below 22°F. Red gum (Eucalyptus camaldulensis) survives 12° to 15°F temperatures and grows to 120' tall. The Silver-dollar gum (Eucalyptus polyanthemos) survives temperatures 14° to 18°F and is a medium-size tree growing to 60' tall. The lemon-scented gum (Eucalyptus citriodora) survives temperatures to 25°F and has a distinctive scent different from the typical odor of the eucalyptus trees. Red-flowering gum (Eucalyptus ficifolia) survives temperatures to 30°F, sometimes lower, has spectacular flowers, and grows to about 40' tall. Red or pink ironbark (Eucalyptus Sideroxylon) has the tough bark typical of the ironbark group of eucalyptus. The gum-type eucalyptus is smooth-barked and often peeling.

Ficus, the ornamental fig tree, includes many evergreen species, some suitable for outdoor cultivation. The best known ficus is probably the commonly-potted Ficus benjamina, the weeping fig; and one of the handsomest evergreen outdoor types is the weeping Chinese banyan, a warm-climate species native to India. Two interesting species with different shapes and uses are described in the paragraphs following.

Ficus rubiginosa, a good potting plant that grows into a wide-spreading tree. It forms aerial roots that eventually become secondary trunks, and its leaves are thick and leathery with rust-colored hairs beneath. The fruit of Ficus rubiginosa is a fig 1/2'' in size and warty in texture. Zone 10.

Ficus macrophylla, the Moreton Bay fig, is a huge evergreen suited to Zone 10. Although tender when young, the Moreton Bay fig acquires hardiness with age and grows into a massive specimen with widely-spreading branches. It produces small, purple, white-spotted figs. It is a tree for the large, warm-climate landscape, and one to plant for posterity as it is very long-lived.

Maintenance Program that Keeps Trees Healthy

Trees when mature require less maintenance than many other plants. But they still need water, fertilizer, and some care if they are to flourish.

Some fertilizer should be applied to mature trees early each spring and any time until the beginning of fall. Surface applications are suitable for young trees and can be applied as a double dose of plant food when the grass is being fed. Mature trees require quite a lot of fertilizer. How much? Measure the diameter of the trunk 3' above ground and apply one pound of balanced fertilizer per inch of trunk. If the soil is particularly poor, double the dose. The preferred system for feeding mature trees is to make holes around the trunk to the outer drip line of the branches and to fill the holes with fertilizer. Garden centers sell tools that make the job easier—for instance, a hollow pipe which removes a core of soil, and can be used as a tube to pour fertilizer back down into the hole. Drip line around the tree is easier to determine when it rains. Ring the tree with holes, spaced 18'' apart, from the drip line to within 1' of the trunk.

Once trees are established and growing they require watering only in severe droughts and after feeding. Trees that are well fed and watered in times of need can fight most of their enemies themselves. However, it is a good idea to check your trees in early spring, at mid-summer, and again in fall for signs of trouble, particularly if the neighborhood trees are having problems. When you spot dead or diseased branches, prune them out and burn. Rake all leaves of trees showing signs of trouble and burn them.

Rabbits and other small, wild creatures feed in winter on the bark of certain trees. They rarely cause much damage to mature specimens, but can be troublesome to newly-set trees. Taping the lower trunk is a good idea if there are furry, little pests in your neighborhood.

The easiest way to get rid of tree fallout in autumn is with a sweeper. Leaves of healthy trees should go into a compost pile; to burn them is to waste natural organic materials and is probably against the law. It is important to remove leaves from under mature shade trees; otherwise leaves kill grass and other plants and tend to result in compacted soil which chokes water and air away from tree rootlets.

Many young trees that will be hardy when mature require winter protection when newly set. This is especially true in regions where high winds and cold weather are the rule. Simplest protection is burlap stapled to 2'' stakes pointed at one end and pounded into the ground before winter sets in.

How and When to Plant Trees

Fall and early winter are the best times to plant trees in mild and warm winter regions. In the North, it is wiser to plant in spring, particularly if very bad winter snow, ice, and wind conditions prevail, as these may destroy limbs and uproot young plants.

Pruning. *1. First undercut limb away from the trunk, as shown. 2. Make top cut to remove limb cleanly. 3. Make flush cut to remove stub. This system keeps limb from tearing bark and damaging the tree.*

The most important step in the planting process is to keep stock from drying out after it arrives from the nursery. Don't expose the roots to wind or sun. Heel in trees that you cannot immediately plant. Dig a trench in a well-drained, protected spot. Separate trees and spread roots and the lower part of the stems against the sloping side of the trench. Cover the roots with about 6'' of moist, well-packed soil. Keep well watered and shaded.

Do not plant shade trees too deeply because a tree breathes through its roots. Dig a hole deep enough to contain roots without crowding or bending. Separate the good topsoil from the poorer bottom soil and break up the subsoil at the bottom of the hole. Mix a thin layer of complete fertilizer and several inches of peat moss into the subsoil and cover the subsoil with several inches of topsoil before planting the tree.

Before planting, prune away any unusually long or broken roots. Spread the roots over a hump of soil in the bottom of the hole and set the tree at the exact level at which it was growing in the nursery. The soil surface line is fairly obvious on young trees. Fill half the hole with good topsoil. Shake the tree to settle the roots, then pack the soil firmly with your feet. This is an important step. Some gardeners poke a rake handle down into the soil to make sure any empty pockets are removed. After the soil is packed, grasp the tree trunk and shake gently to make sure it really is firmly set. If it seems loose, prod the soil again with a rake handle and pack once more with your feet. Fill the hole around the tree with water.

When water has soaked in, fill the hole with topsoil, leaving a slight depression to catch rain. Pack the soil once more with your feet. Water again and allow water to drain through. Water twice more, in the same way.

Spacing ornamental trees is as important as proper planting. Large-growing trees such as cottonwood and maples should be spaced 30' to 50' apart; 25' to 40' should be allowed between trees of medium height, such as Redmond linden and Moraine ash. Spacing is a matter of judgment, and trees may be set somewhat closer if need be.

After planting, cut back side branches of new trees one half their length. Do not cut the main stem but remove any leaders that could divert growth into double trunks. Any branch forming too sharp a crotch with the main stem is inviting disaster from heavy snows and should be cut out.

Newly-planted shade trees over 6' tall may require staking. It is a sound safety measure to leave trees staked for about a year. Drive a sturdy stake into the ground beside the tree. Tie the tree to the stake in several places. Wind burlap or an odd bit of garden hose around rope or wire to prevent cutting into the tree trunk.

Other than a preliminary, light pruning at planting time, shade trees usually are left alone, save for removing dead or damaged limbs.

With the exception of the elms, limbs forming a bad crotch should be eliminated. Unless absolutely necessary, it is unwise to prune shade trees when the sap is flowing. Some, particularly maple, birch, and elm, "bleed" profusely. Summer pruning after leaves have developed is the best time to prune this type of tree. Flowering peach and crab apples are best pruned during the dormant winter months. Don't leave any stubs; they are ugly and invite decay. Use a sharp saw; cut the branch clean at the trunk. You won't tear the bark if you remove the branch in sections.

Watering is the most important part of planting. Water newly-planted trees regularly and thoroughly until vigorous growth shows that the trees are on their own and flourishing. When you water, soak the soil thoroughly; remember, you have to wet all the soil right down to the bottom root. A steady but gentle flow from the garden hose is the best system since it won't wash the soil away.

3•Shrubs for All-Year Garden Beauty

Shrubs, along with vines and the small flowering trees, are important design elements in landscape planning. They are both permanent and large. Like key subjects in a painting, they draw the eye, anchoring flower borders, outlining lawn and boundaries, softening harsh elements such as the bare facades of modern architecture, and screening out undesirable elements. The landscape will be balanced or lopsided, serene or busy, dull or exciting according to shrub selection or placement.

The shrub design "dont's" are simple: too many shrubs, vines, and small trees in one section unbalances the whole; too many in a small landscape may make it too busy to be serene; all of one kind dulls the view and robs the garden of seasonal change, its major charm. The materials in the shrub category are many: there are leaf-losing (deciduous) types and evergreens, flowering and non-flowering, and shrubs with foliage of every kind from tiny on twiggy branches, spirea for instance, to majestic and evergreen, such as rhododendron. For every climate and situation there are outstanding shrubs that combine to bring beauty to the landscape, whether it is country acreage or a city terrace.

A flowering shrub has a double purpose—to add color to the garden in its two-to-four-week blooming period, and to bring structure and texture to the painting that is a landscape during the other months. Keep both of these characteristics in mind as you plan. Shape and branching habit are especially important in deciduous flowering shrubs because these are the elements that will stand out when winter comes and leaves fall.

Exuberant, no-problem shrubs such as forsythia soften corners with their luxuriant growth, create thickets if left unpruned, make casual hedges, and give medium-tall screening. The forsythia's brilliant, early-spring flowers are also easy to force into winter bloom simply by cutting some of the branches and bringing them indoors; place in a deep vase of water.

Dainty, twiggy shrubs such as the tiny-leaved spirea or bridal-wreath bring airiness to borders of bold shrubs and evergreens. And tall subjects, such as the beautybush, are large enough to set alone as specimens in the lawn and to use as screening at property boundaries.

In addition to plant structure and size, each species has a distinct style or mood, and many have especially desirable characteristics. When planning new plantings, or revamping an older garden, make sure your shrub additions bring new interest and fit harmoniously into the existing landscape.

Layered angular branches of *Japanese quince* suggest the Orient. Japanese (or flowering) quince is prolific with blooms but gives fruit fit only for birds. True quince has fewer flowers but produces the fruit from which quince jellies and jams are made. Flowering quince may be planted in hedge rows and trimmed, or used as a single specimen. Branches are fine for forcing, as described for forsythia.

Old-fashioned *lilac*, a tree-tall shrub, brings with it a nostalgic charm and has highly fragrant flowers. Modern French hybrids have handsome foliage and single or double flowers in white, pink, lavender, dark blue, or claret purple, but may be less fragrant. Decaisne is the variety to plant if you need a broad, not tall, lilac. Lilacs need soil on the alkaline side; they should not be combined with evergreen plants which require acid soils.

Bold *hydrangea* fills corners with the solid mass of its strong, green leaves during the growing season and bursts into spectacular and long-lasting bloom in midseason. A wonderful seaside subject, the hydrangea also makes a handsome hedge plant. Flowers are white, pink, or blue. Some pinks go blue, or vice versa, depending on the acid-alkaline content of the soil, but whites are always white. Desirable pH for pinks is 6.0 to 6.5 (see page 29). To increase blueness, add aluminum sulfate, one pound per seven gallons of water.

The *tree peony* is one of the plants whose bloom is so glorious, it is grown entirely for its flowers. An imposing shrub only after many years, it demands a prominent location from the very beginning, and is usually treated as a specimen, that is, set off alone. Tree peonies are not as tough as common peonies, and they tend to sulk when first planted.

Sweet mock-orange is grown for its intensely fragrant flowers. The sweetest types are generally 7' to 9' tall and should be featured as specimens or grown as a medium-tall screening thicket or hedge.

Camellia, a tall shrub or small flowering tree, is grown for its handsome evergreen foliage and extraordinarily-beautiful, symmetrically-perfect flowers. Blooming period is late fall, winter, or earliest spring, depending on region and variety. In cold, cold climates, only for a cool sun porch or greenhouse.

Witch-hazel is another late-winter, earliest-spring bloomer. Its shaggy, red-tinged yellow blooms are a delight seen against late winter snow. It thrives in filtered light at woodland's edge, but also survives in city conditions.

Snowball blossoms recall old-fashioned gardens and bloom in summer or late spring. A highly fragrant species is Viburnum carlcephalum. A new snowball, the viburnum named Juddi, even more fragrant, produces its faintly pink blossoms in early spring.

Summer lilac and *butterfly bush* are names for buddleia, a fragrant, early-summer bloomer attractive to butterflies. A fountain of bloom, it makes a splendid lawn specimen and is attractive as a backdrop for flower borders. The flowers are also wonderful for cutting to enjoy in bouquets indoors.

The *rhododendrons,* many of them known as *azaleas,* include both evergreen and deciduous types. All are glorious when they bloom in spring or early summer. The rhododendrons generally have the largest, boldest leaves, while azalea foliage tends to a finer texture. Evergreen types are among the most desirable of foundation shrubs.

Mature rhododendrons stage a fabulous display. These shrubs will reach the size of small trees. Rhododendrons are excellent in tubs for city terraces, and the azalea types even flourish in indoor gardens where soil is humusy, acid, moist, and the air has enough humidity.

Flowering evergreen shrubs are ideal where the landscape will benefit from winter-long greenery. Select according to color of the blossoms, blooming time, size, and texture of the leaves. Borders of evergreen flowering shrubs are most interesting when small- and large-leafed, tall- and low-growing varieties are combined. Be aware that some evergreen plants in warmer areas may lose leaves and branch tips in colder regions, especially in years when snow cover is lacking. English lavender, whose small, grayish foliage survives cold if covered by snow, is typical. Many of these sometimes tender evergreens make excellent house plants. Most of the evergreen shrubs, except the conifers or needled evergreens, have some type of bloom, but only a few have really outstanding flowers. Most evergreens need some acidity in the soil and a well-drained site.

Feathery heather, a tiny-leaved flowering evergreen, is one of the most attractive and useful low-growing types. It hazes over with small, subtly-shaded blossoms in summer or early fall. A superb plant for gardens by the sea.

Spring-blooming *mountain-laurel*, whose lovely pale pink blossoms are reminiscent of rhododendrons, needs dappled shade and a naturalized situation but will flourish in foundation plantings and borders if given an acid, humusy soil, and some protection from hot sun.

Fragrant *gardenias* are suited only to warmer climates outdoors but thrive as house plants in colder areas. The exquisitely scented, creamy-white flowers appear in summer and are backed by shiny, dark-green leaves.

There are two principal categories of evergreen shrubs planted to green the landscape—the needle evergreens (conifers) such as juniper, and the small-to-medium-leafed types, such as Japanese holly, boxwood, pyracantha, andromeda, evergreen euonymus, and some of the new and exciting barberries. Many varieties in each category bear bright berries or other fruit in the fall. These are the shrubs used to fill low, empty spaces between maturing rhododendrons, to set under high-branching trees meant to screen the road or neighboring property, as backdrops for flower borders, and for hedges that are green year round. In the needled category the most versatile shrubs are probably the yew, which has intensely green leaves and an upright growth habit, and juniper, whose foliage tends to blue-gray and sprawls casually, and arbor-vitae, whose green is lighter, sometimes yellowed, when a tall evergreen is required. All of these come in dwarf, medium, and tall varieties.

Shrubs With Special Purpose: Hedges

Shrubs for formal hedges can be anything from privet to species of forsythia, providing the plants used grow slowly through the season and aren't damaged by the constant pruning required to keep a formal hedge

RIGHT   WRONG
Keep base of hedge bush wider than the top.

in shape. Common shrubs for formal hedges are the trimmable and slow-growing English or the hardier Korean boxwood, privet, and the several varieties of yew, a well-behaved, needled evergreen.

Shrubs for informal hedges of various heights can be all of these if they are allowed to grow freely without being trimmed to formal squared or rounded shapes. Privet grows very tall and produces masses of delicate, creamy-white blossoms when it is uncut. Evergreen euonymus and Japanese holly are excellent for hedges and there's a leaf-losing corkbush dwarf that flames red in fall, making a beautiful hedge. Hybrid polyanthus roses that bloom all summer, yellow, red, and burgundy-leafed barberries, the dwarf bluish arctic willow, Cotoneaster divaricata, and many other flowering and colorful leafed shrubs are excellent material for hedging.

Primary Rule for Planting Shrubs: Dig a Big Hole

Evergreens, particularly larger plants, are usually sold with a ball of earth clinging to the roots, and more soil packed tightly around the ball, held in place by a burlap bag or container. A shrub or tree thus readied for transplanting is said to be balled and burlapped ("B&B") or container-grown.

Planting a balled-and-burlapped shrub

1. Never lift a balled-and-burlapped shrub by its top; use a large burlap bag or canvas sheet to slide the plant into the planting hole.

2. Measure the ball of roots with a ruler or a board and dig a hole twice its width and one-and-a-half times its depth. Mix in 3" of peat moss in the bottom. Add dug-out soil mixed with more peat moss to the bottom of the hole until it measures the exact depth of root ball.

3. Use burlap or canvas to ease the plant into the prepared planting hole.

4. Pack dug-out soil into the hole until two-thirds of the root ball is covered. Cut the ropes around the root ball, loosen burlap, then fill the hole with water. When it has drained away fill the hole to old-soil mark on trunk. Make a 2"-high saucer around planting hole to hold water. Fill hole with water. Until the plant is established, water daily or several times a week.

Planting a container-grown shrub

1. Several hours before planting, add enough water to moisten soil without soaking it. Dig a hole and prepare soil as directed for balled-and-burlapped plants.

2. When the planting hole is ready, loosen the container and slide out the root ball, taking care to keep the ball of earth intact around roots.

3. Use hands to loosen without breaking the roots around the ball of soil. Straighten roots to their full length.

4. Plant and water as directed for balled-and-burlapped shrubs.

Planting Deciduous Shrubs

Leaf-losing shrubs are most often shipped during their dormant season in the cold months when branches are leafless. Because at this season there

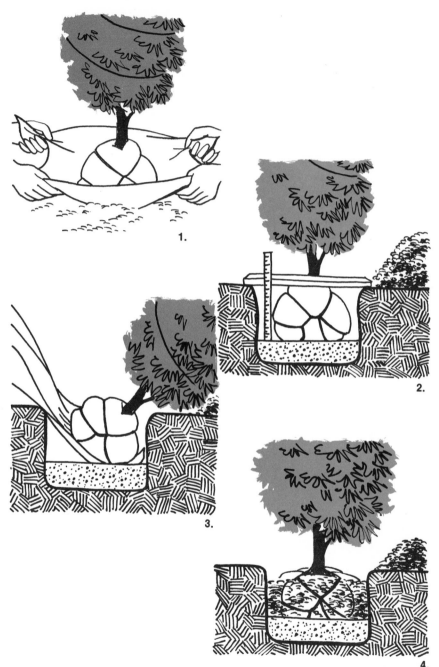

Planting a balled-and-burlapped shrub. Follow directions on page 75.

Planting a container-grown shrub. Follow directions on page 75.

are no leaves that require moisture and nourishment of the roots, the shrubs often are sold bare-root, that is, without soil.

Planting a bare-root shrub

1. Dig a hole and prepare soil as directed for balled-and-burlapped shrub planting. Mound the soil in the bottom of the hole slightly and spread bare shrub roots over the mound.

2. Fill the hole three-quarters full with prepared soil removed from the planting hole and tamp firmly with the heel of your hand or your foot, if the shrub is large. Fill the hole with water and, when it has drained, fill to the top with soil.

3. Build a 2'' saucer of earth around the hole to hold water. Fill with water and allow to drain.

4. Prune away one-third of the branch tips. This helps compensate for roots lost when the plant was dug at the nursery. Use this pruning to help shape the eventual form of the shrub.

40 Shrubs for Green Survival

KEY TO SYMBOLS
Hardiness
Z for zone-range adaptability (see map on page 38); ''a'' indicates northern, colder limits and ''b'' indicates southern, warmer limits
Height at Maturity
T for tall, above 6'/**M** for medium, 3'-6'/**D** for dwarf, below 3'
Decorative or Other Values
1 for showy flowers/**2** for ornamental fruits/**3** for evergreen or interesting foliage/**4** for fall foliage color/**5** for suitable light shade

Abelia grandiflora (Glossy abelia)—Z 6b-10a, M, 1, 3
Acanthopanax sieboldianus (Aralia)—Z 5b-8a, T, 3, 5
Arbutus unedo (Strawberry-tree)—Z 8-10, T, 2, 3
Aronia arbutifolia (Red chokeberry)—Z 4-9a, T, 1, 2, 4
Berberis thunbergii (Japanese barberry)—Z 3-10a, M, 2
Buxus microphylla japonica (Japanese boxwood)—Z 6-10a, M, 3, 5
Camellia japonica (in variety)(Camellia)—Z 7-10a, T, 1, 3, 5
Chionanthus virginicus (Fringetree)—Z 5-10a, T, 1, 2, 4 ·
Clethra alnifolia (Summersweet)—Z 3b-9, T, 1, 4
Deutzia gracilis (Slender deutzia)—Z 5-8, D, 1
Elaeagnus angustifolia (Russian-olive)—Z 3-9, T, 2, 3
Euonymus alatus (Burning bush)—Z 3b-10a, T, 2, 3, 4
Forsythia intermedia (Forsythia)—Z 5b-8, T, 1

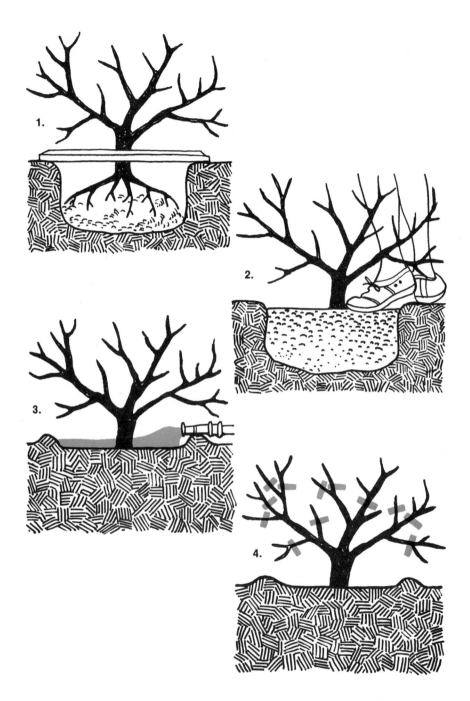

Planting a bare-root shrub. Follow directions on page 78.

Fothergilla monticola (Alabama fothergilla)—Z 5-9, M, 1
Hamamelis mollis (Chinese witch-hazel)—Z 6-9, T, 1
Hibiscus rosa-sinensis (Chinese hibiscus)—Z 9-10, T, 1, 3
Hibiscus syriacus (Shrub althea)—Z 5b-10a, T, 1
Hypericum patulum henryi (Henry St. John's-wort)—Z 7b-10, D, 1, 3
Ilex crenata (Japanese holly)—Z 6b-9, T, 3, 5
Juniperus chinensis Pfitzeriana (Pfitzer juniper)—Z 4-10, M, 3
Kalmia latifolia (Mountain-laurel)—Z 5-9a, T, 1, 3, 5
Kolkwitzia amabilis (Beauty bush)—Z 5-9, T, 1, 2
Lagerstroemia indica (Crape-myrtle)—Z 7-9, T/M, 1, 3, 4
Lonicera tatarica (Tatarian honeysuckle)—Z 3-8, T, 1
Nerium oleander (Oleander)—Z 8b-10, T, 1, 3
Philadelphus coronarius (Mock-orange)—Z 4b-9a, T, 1
Pieris japonica (Japanese andromeda)—Z 6-9, M, 1
Pittosporum tobira (Japanese pittosporum)—Z 8-10, T, 1
Potentilla fruticosa (Bush cinquefoil)—Z 2b-9, M, 1, 3
Raphiolepis indica (India hawthorn)—Z 8-10, M, 1, 2, 3
Rhododendron (in variety)(Rhododendron and azalea)—Z 4-9, T/M/D, 1, 3, 4, 5
Rhodotypos scandens (Jetbead)—Z 5-9a, M, 1, 2, 3, 4
Rhus copallina (Shining sumac)—Z 5-9, T, 2, 3, 4
Rosa rugosa (Rugosa rose)—Z 3-8, M, 1, 2, 3, 4
Spiraea bumalda (Bumalda spirea)—Z 4-9a, D, 1, 3
Spiraea vanhouttei (Vanhoutte spirea)—Z 4-10a, M, 1, 4
Taxus cuspidata (Japanese yew)—Z 5-8, T/M, 2, 3, 5
Virburnum carlcephalum (Fragrant snowball)—Z 5b-10a, T, 1, 2, 3
Viburnum plicatum Mariesii (Marie's doublefile viburnum)—Z 5b-8, T, 1, 2, 3, 4
Xanthorhiza simplicissima (Yellow-root)—Z 5-9, D, 3, 5

4•Vines for Flowers, Shade and Screening

Vines are versatile. You will find the solution to many landscape problems through the thoughtful use of vines. Vines serve as screens, ground covers, and they hide unsightly walls and fences. They may be an excellent source of cut flowers and, best of all, they provide plenty of summer color. And they needn't take up much space.

As screens, vines give needed privacy; as ground covers, they help stabilize loose banks and hide unsightly bare spots; as wall and fence covers, they soften and lessen the ugly intrusion of woven steel, aluminum, and concrete into the natural surroundings of your home; and vines will give color in the landscape in all seasons.

Most vines are either annual or penennial in habit. The annuals are those that grow from seed to bloom in a single season, providing quick shading, screening, or ground cover. Some of the best annual vines include Cobaea scandens (cathedral bells), cypress vine, marble vine, Thunbergia alata (black-eyed-Susan-vine), morning-glory, Scarlet Runner bean, and sweet pea.

Outstanding Perennial Vines

Bittersweet (Celastrus scandens). Zones 4 to 10. Bittersweet is a good choice for bank planting. It will also climb walls and other supports and it thrives in ordinary garden soil. It often reaches a height of 35'. Small, yellow flowers appear in the summer, followed by orange-colored fruits in the fall. Bittersweet has male and female flowers that are borne on separate plants. You must have the female plant to bear fruit and the male for pollination. American bittersweet and oriental bittersweet are the most used and are readily available at nurseries.

Clematis. This vine can be difficult to grow, but its beauty makes it well worth some special effort. If you attempt to grow clematis, it may be a good idea to consult with a local gardening authority, perhaps someone at a nursery or garden center. Most gardeners have trouble with clematis because it requires a limestone, alkaline soil.

Clematis flowers range from wine-red to pure white, and come in many shapes—bells, urns, saucers, and stars. Some are as small as 1'', others are as large as 10'' across. The plants vary in size from 5' to 50', according to variety. Some species bloom on last year's wood and some bloom on the current season's growth. If you plant the former, prune the plants only after they flower; if the latter, you can prune (severely, if you want) early in the spring. The species presented here are those that will add color to the garden in all seasons, but especially in summer.

Sweet Autumn Clematis. Zones 5 to 10. Sweet autumn clematis bears small, white flowers in late August. It blooms on the current year's growth and is by far the most common and vigorous clematis. It has very dark foliage and fragrant flowers, is very easy to grow, and it is excellent for use as a screen. It usually grows 10' to 15' tall, but will often reach 30' on a warm wall.

Anemone-flowered Clematis. Zones 6 to 10. Anemone-flowered clematis is a hybrid with medium-size flowers that appear in June and July. Colors are white, pink, or red. It blooms on the previous year's wood.

Scarlet Clematis. Zones 4 to 8. This distinctive Texas species bears urn-shaped flowers in July. It grows about 6' tall. Its main period of bloom is in July, but it will flower sporadically until frost. Scarlet clematis frequently dies back to the ground in winter, but sprouts again the following spring. It blooms on the current year's growth.

Jackman Clematis. Zones 6 to 10. Jackman clematis is one of the most popular. It blooms in mid-July and the flowers are violet-purple, 5'' to 7'' in diameter. Since it blooms on the current year's wood, it can be heavily pruned early in the spring.

Plant in spring in alkaline soil or a light, loamy soil to which lime has been added. The plant should be in a spot where the top portion receives sun or dappled shade but the roots can remain cool. String or other narrow support is necessary because the vine climbs by twisting its leaf stalk around the support.

Many large, flowering, hybrid clematis are available. A few plants of each variety will provide lasting summer color.

Variety	Color
Prins Hendric	Azure blue
Crimson Star	Dark red
Lord Neville	Dark plum
Comtesse de Bouchaud	Rose
Duchess of Edinburgh	White

Set the plants out in early spring or fall. Plant in a moist, rich, alkaline soil that is well drained. The roots need a cool, shady spot. If winters are severe, it is safer to plant only in the spring. Set the collar of the plant about 2'' below the surface. Guide the new stems with string until they reach the wall or trellis. When starting young clematis, it is a good idea to train them to grow fan-wise. If you don't, you'll end up with a tangled mass of unmanageable foliage. Screen the main stem of each plant from pets. A hungry puppy can quickly do a great deal of damage.

Honeysuckle (Lonicera). There are many varieties of honeysuckle, but only a few are suitable for adding summer color to your garden. While the two species presented here are not the only ones suitable, they have been chosen because they are relatively easy to grow, they bloom over a long period, and are hardy over most of the United States. Honeysuckle is very ornamental and grows 15' to 20' tall.

Set your plants out in the early spring or fall. Honeysuckle does best in full sun, but will withstand partial shade. For a fence, screen, or trellis, set the plants about 2' apart.

Hall's Honeysuckle. Zones 5 to 9. Hall's honeysuckle grows taller than the everblooming variety, often as high as 20'. It makes a very good ground cover. The flowers appear in midsummer and continue until fall. They are dark yellow and white and are very fragrant. This species can often be seen growing in the woods in Zones 6 and 7, where it is a nuisance.

Sweet Honeysuckle. Zones 6 to 9. This species is the most fragrant of all the honeysuckles. The flowers appear in early June and are white to pale yellow, trumpet-shaped, about 2'' long.

Silver Fleece Vine (Polygonum aubertii). Zones 5 to 10. Silver fleece vine is sometimes called the Silver lace vine. The flowers appear in August. They form dense clusters and are white, pale green, or pink. This vine often reaches a height of 20' to 30'.

Trumpet Vine (Campsis radicans). Zones 4 to 10. Trumpet vine flowers in July. The flowers are orange to scarlet, trumpet shaped, and about 2'' in diameter. Trumpet vine has large leaves and it will reach a height of 30' on a warm wall. Trumpet vine clings by small, root-like holdfasts. It is rampant and soon becomes very heavy. Trumpet vine grows in almost any soil in full sun. Plant only where there is plenty of room for the vine to spread.

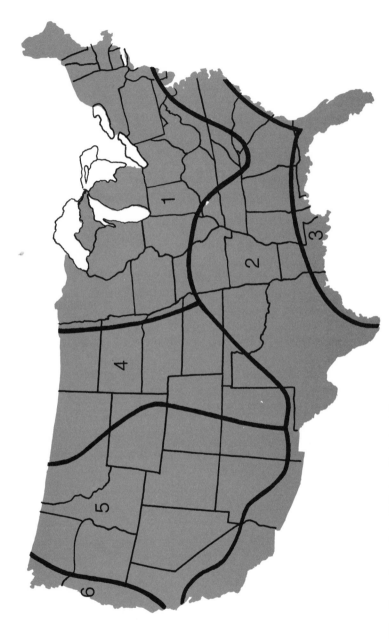

Climatic regions of the U.S. in which the following grasses are suitable for lawns: Region 1. Common Kentucky bluegrass, Merion Kentucky bluegrass, red fescue, and Colonial bentgrass. Tall fescue, bermudagrass, and zoysiagrass in southern portion of the region. Region 2. Bermudagrass and zoysiagrass. Centipedegrass, carpetgrass, and St. Augustinegrass in southern portion of the region with tall fescue and Kentucky bluegrass in some northern areas. Region 3. St. Augustinegrass, bermudagrass, zoysiagrass, carpetgrass, and bahiagrass. Region 4. Nonirrigated areas: Crested wheatgrass, buffalograss, and blue gramagrass. Irrigated areas: Kentucky bluegrass and red fescue. Region 5. Nonirrigated areas: Crested wheatgrass. Irrigated areas: Kentucky bluegrass and red fescue. Region 6. Colonial bentgrass and Kentucky bluegrass.

5•How to Have a Great Lawn (Without Being its Slave)

Today's approach to lawnkeeping is that man is master, and while natural elements can make it difficult at times, having a perfectly manicured, evenly-green lawn is a highly satisfying experience. Especially when it is newly green after rain, fragrant when freshly cut on a summer evening, or when you stroll through it barefoot. The way to a beautiful lawn is to start with the best grass you can buy. Feed it well, mow frequently, and invest in an underground sprinkler system that will water the lawn automatically, even when you are away.

Growing a lawn is like raising any other living organism. The initial cost of the grass is relatively minor when you consider the expense of maintenance year after year. Vigorous turf grows out of a continuing program of care and feeding. To get the most value for your investment of time and money, start with the best grass you can afford. Ironically, a bad lawn requires more effort than a good one. A healthy, dense turf will prevent weeds from multiplying and fend off other forms of pest and disease.

Grass breeders are constantly working toward varieties that naturally grow low and slowly so that mowing is required less frequently. At the same time, they are looking for disease resistance and greater tolerance of extremes in temperature and moisture.

Fylking and Windsor are two fairly new bluegrasses. They are available now in seed or sod. Originally from northern Europe, Fylking is amazingly resistant to all diseases. It is low growing and can be clipped as closely as 1/2''. Windsor is greener, thicker, and sturdier than other bluegrasses, yet it requires less mowing. Windsor stands up well in heat and drought; when seeded into an existing lawn, it will eventually take over, simply crowding out less-vigorous strains. The newest fescues are Highlight and Oasis. Both form a dense sod with erect growth that can be kept closely clipped. The color, texture, and growth habit is such that either variety can be used alone in full sun, or in dry, shaded situations, and in mixtures with bluegrass.

The best grass for you depends on where you live and how your lawn will be used. Wherever northern or cool-season grasses are grown, most lawns are either all bluegrass, or a mixture of bluegrass and fine fescues. Solid bentgrass is common on the golf course and sometimes is used for a home lawn where intensive care is possible. It is not desirable to mix bentgrass with bluegrass, except possibly in a shaded situation. Red fescues and Poa trivialis are also used in shade. For rough-and-tumble play or low-maintenance utility lawns, the tall fescues like Alta and Kentucky 31 are excellent. In arid, cold climates, crested wheatgrass and buffalograss are used. Redtop, a bentgrass that doesn't creep, and ryegrass are short-lived, coarse grasses often used for quick cover on a new lawn until the arrival of a better time to sow permanent grass. Perennial rye gets off to a fast start, probably its only desirable feature, and eventually bunches into clumps. Annual ryegrass, also called domestic or Italian, is coarser and lives only one season.

Starting a New Lawn

A number of factors determine whether you seed or sod a lawn. Soil preparation is the same for either. Seed of improved varieties is more widely distributed than sod of the same quality. Seed is less expensive initially, but more vulnerable to adverse weather, which can make reseeding necessary. Good sod is more costly in the beginning, but it is also more tolerant of less than perfect conditions and better able to compete with weeds. Sod is the way to have a beautiful lawn immediately, or to use for quick repair of bare places in established turf, provided you can match color and texture. Sod is easier to establish than seed on a steep incline, or in any other situation where erosion by wind or water is a problem.

When you buy lawn seed, read the label on the box carefully to be sure it contains the kind of grass you want. Some mixtures are clearly marked for specific purposes, such as utility, play, or shade. Coarse grasses like annual rye for quick cover are inexpensive. High-quality perennial grass seeds are never, repeat *never*, cheap. If the price seems unusually low, double check the label. Occasionally, cut-rate packages imply that they are predominately a selected bluegrass, such as Merion, when in reality they contain only a token amount, maybe no more than 1%.

The best time to start a new lawn from seed is late August or early September. Early spring is next. Sodding is possible at almost any time the weather permits putting it down. To establish a new lawn from seed:

1. Level and grade the ground.
2. Prepare soil to a depth of 4'' to 6''; if it is poor subsoil, enrich with peat moss or compost.
3. To each 1000 square feet of area apply 50 to 75 pounds ground dolomitic limestone and 30 to 40 pounds superphosphate. Work these into the top 4'' to 6'' of soil. A soil pH of 6.5 is desirable.
4. Rake the surface smooth, then apply 10-6-4, 10-10-10, or a similar lawn fertilizer.

5. Seed permanent grass at the rate suggested on the container for a new lawn. Sow seeds with a spreader for even distribution, applying half one way, half at right angles. Rake lightly to cover. Mulch with a thin covering of straw or peat moss. Keep constantly moist by sprinkling two or three times daily until the new grass is growing actively.

If you have a lawn that is less than satisfactory, it is probably worth upgrading if it contains at least 40% to 50% desirable, perennial grasses. Otherwise, you will be wise to banish the existing turf and start over as for a new lawn.

If you decide to save your established lawn, the most direct way to upgrade is to put all of your budget in fertilizer and concentrate your efforts on frequent mowing and adequate watering. This upgrading program can be intensified by using weedkillers and seeding with an improved variety like Windsor. Upgrading indicates a gradual but definite improvement program, and it can be started at any time grass is making active growth.

If the lawn to be upgraded has uneven areas that need grading or leveling, late summer and early fall are the ideal times to bring in the necessary topsoil and then sow seeds.

A Program for Lawn Renovation

A more ambitious renovation program is best begun in late August or early September. These are the steps to follow:

1. Apply 2,4-D to kill broadleaf weeds. If crabgrass is a serious problem, make two or three applications of DSMA or MSMA at least three weeks before seeding.
2. Rent a lawn aerator to loosen the soil without ruining the existing grass.
3. Use a soil-test kit to determine the pH, or have this done through your county Cooperative Extension Agent. If the pH is below 6.5, apoply 50 to 75 pounds of ground agricultural limestone per 100 square feet.
4. In September, apply a well-balanced lawn fertilizer.
5. Rake bare areas to loosen soil, then seed perennial grasses at a rate of one to two pounds per 1000 square feet. Rake lightly.
6. Keep the soil moist until seedlings become established. This may require sprinkling two or three times daily in the early stages.
7. During this time continue regular mowing.

Never underestimate the power of adequate feeding in building and maintaining a lawn. Bluegrass needs four feedings a year, spaced approximately in October, November, May, and June; Merion needs six feedings. Fescues do well on only two, October and April. Today's lawn fertilizers, when applied according to directions on the package, offer very little threat of burning. Many have a slow-release feature that helps to give uniform growth from feeding to feeding.

Lawn Watering Tips

In the absence of sufficient rainfall, the rule is to water deeply—to a depth of about 6''—and not again until the grass first shows signs of wilting. Avoid frequent, shallow sprinkling because this encourages surface rooting and increases the possibility of disease. Contrary to widespread belief, it is not harmful to water at night.

In an average season, there isn't a lawn in America that doesn't need supplementary watering. Unless you live in an unusually wet climate, the best way to accomplish this is by installing one of the underground sprinkling systems available today. These include a timer that can be set to water the lawn automatically, even when you are away.

When you mow your lawn, be sure the cutting blade is sharp. Otherwise it will cut unevenly, literally chewing off and damaging the grass. Mow frequently, so that no more than 1/4 to 1/3 of the leaf surface is removed at any given time. Grass kept at 1'' to 1½'' should have no more than 1/2'' removed at a given mowing. In very hot weather, leave the grass about an inch longer than usual. In the fall, mow until freeze-up so that the grass doesn't go into winter so tall that it mats.

Use a mower large enough to accomplish the job in reasonable time. If you have anything approaching an acre or more in grass, use a rider or tractor-type mower. Today's best mowers of all types have key electric starting so that they can be turned on as easily as a car.

When grass is growing actively, catch and remove the clippings. This helps avoid the buildup of thatch that can eventually prevent water and food from reaching grass roots.

While some kind of mower—power or hand-powered—is necessary for trimming large areas of lawn grass, for all of the difficult spots, where such a metal-bladed cutting instrument cannot reach, use a string-line trimmer such as the Needie®. Not only is a string-line trimmer totally safe, it eliminates hours of tedious, hard work and will enable you to keep your lawn neatly manicured all season—with the same enthusiasm in September as you feel on the first nice day in spring when you are finally able to get out of the house and into the great outdoors.

Coping With Lawn Weeds

Weedkillers, or herbicides, are invaluable in the building and maintenance of a lawn but they can never substitute for correct cultural practices. However, if your lawn seems to be so crowded with weeds that there is no place for grass to expand, a weedkiller is in order.

Most broadleaf weeds will succumb to an application or two of 2,4-D. Use Silvex (2,4,5-TP) for such stubborn weeds as wild onion, chickweed, henbit, and white clover (if you consider it a weed). Dicamba is best for controlling sheep sorrel, creeping spurge, and knotweed. Apply when growth is active, on days that are generally warm and sunny. Early fall is one excellent time, especially in crabgrass country; spring-killed broadleaf weeds leave a place for crabgrass to grow; fall-killed weeds give grass time to grow before the crabgrass. Otherwise, spring is an excellent time to apply weedkillers.

Stop crabgrass early. Where crabgrass is a problem, use one of the pre-emergent controls in early spring, before crabgrass begins to sprout. You will find a supply of these at your local lawn and garden center. The chief ingredient may be DCPA (Dacthal), Bensulide, Presan, Betasan, Terbutal, Azak, Siduron, or Tupersan. Only the last two mentioned can be used immediately before, at time of, or immediately after seeding without injury to the lawngrass seedlings.

Post-emergence killers of crabgrass are sold under various trade names at local garden centers in midsummer. They are usually formulations of DSMA or MSMA and treatment will be required two or three times at seven-to-ten-day intervals.

The chemical control of weedy, perennial grasses such as orchard, timothy, quack, and nimblewill is not so simple a matter. The material to use is Dalapon, mixed at the rate of 1/4-pound to 1 gallon of water. Spray individual plants or badly-infested areas. Desirable grasses will also be killed; be as selective as possible with the spray. Dalapon disappears from warm, moist soil in three to six weeks but persists longer in cool or dry soils, after which time good grass can be sown or sodded.

Troublesome insects that inhabit lawns, or destroy them, can be controlled by seasonal applications of lawn insecticides or pesticides available at local garden centers and nurseries. Follow package directions. Use one of these in June to control June beetle grubs and ants. Use Diazinon or Sevin to control chinchbugs and sod webworms.

Growing grass in the shade requires a different approach than growing it without competition in sunny, open ground. Feed at two or three times the normal rate. Water deeply but only when necessary. Maintain pH in favor of the grass; don't let it become extremely acid. Remove overhanging tree branches, to 10' from the ground if possible, and thin above this point as much as is desirable for the health and appearance of the trees. Mow the grass higher than usual. Apply fungicides when disease is noted.

Lawns in the South

Southern or warm-season grasses are usually started in the spring or early summer. Start bermuda, carpet, centipede, and Zoysia japonica from seeds or sprigs. Start Emerald and Meyer zoysias, and St. Augustine, from sprigs. Whenever frosted, these grasses turn quite brown; for green lawns in winter, they can be overseeded in fall with domestic ryegrass, excepting centipede, which forms a turf that is too dense.

Feed Southern grasses at least twice each year, in spring and summer. Remove thatch in the early spring, about the time grass begins to green up. This raking is especially important for heavily-fed lawns where clippings are never caught.

In general, among Southern grasses, carpetgrass needs more water, zoysia and St. Augustine more fertilizer, and centipede requires the least maintenance. Zoysia and St. Augustine are the most shade-tolerant.

There are a number of improved bermudagrasses available. Tifdwarf has tiny leaves that hug the ground; 1/4'' cutting is possible. It is darker green and a little more winter hardy, requires less fertilizer and less mowing than Tifgreen, a larger version. Tiflawn spreads faster than common bermuda and will eventually crowd it out when introduced into an old lawn. Compared to Tifgreen, Tiflawn stays greener longer, is more drought-resistant and shade-tolerant at 2'' and 3'' in height but is not as cold hardy. The hardiest strain of bermuda is U-3, which grows north to Nebraska.

6•Ground Covers for Difficult Places

Grass is the most common ground cover, but there are many others that will grow in places where grass is difficult to handle or simply won't grow. The ground covers have the advantage of requiring no mowing and they bring variety to the garden with their texture and color. Deep shade, rocky or very moist soil, and steep slopes are some of the places where ground covers of one sort or another will succeed where grass will not. The initial cost in labor and money for installing ground covers may be high, but nearly all can be propagated at home easily by division or by rooting in damp sand. Among the most useful and attractive ground covers are these:

Creeping bugleweed (Ajuga reptans) is 2'' to 4'' tall, spreads a carpet of blue flowers in spring. Good in shade as well as sun. For cool and hot regions.

Chamomile (Anthemis nobilis) grows 3'' to 10'' tall, has ferny leaves, tiny daisy-like flowers, and a pungent fragrance when stepped on. Succeeds in sandy soils in most areas of the United States.

Wild ginger (Asarum caudatum) grows 2'' to 6'' tall, thrives in partial shade in moist, slightly acid soils. Good for growing under rhododendrons. Grows well in all regions that aren't extremely cold in winter.

Lily-of-the-valley (Convallaria) has furled, green leaves that choke out weeds and spread. Exquisite fragrance of the bell-shaped flowers makes it a highly desirable ground cover. Grows in partial shade in moist soil in all but warmest regions.

Dichondra repens is often used as lawn material in Arizona and Southern California. Grows only in warmest sections of the country. (Incidentally, dichondra makes a charming hanging plant indoors in a sunny window; be sure to keep the soil moist.)

Purple wintercreeper (Euonymus) is an evergreen vine that forms a 6''-high carpet. Grows in full sun or light shade, but only in temperate to warm areas.

Wild strawberry (Fragaria chiloensis) grows 6'' to 12'' tall, bears tiny white flowers and miniscule fruit. Good along the West Coast in full sun or light shade. Suitable for cover on sand dunes.

Algerian or English ivies (Hedera) make handsome ground cover of 6'' to 8'' and some species are hardy in most areas of the country. Most thrive in deep shade or full sun, as long as they are provided with moist, rich soil.

Baby's-tears (Helxine) is about 1'' tall, has tiny leaves, forms a dense, soft cushion; used as ground cover in warmer zones. It succeeds in light or even in deep shade; needs moist, rich soil. (Another ground cover that makes a wonderful house plant.)

Pachysandra terminalis is probably the most commonly used ground cover in America's temperate regions. Grows to 6'' tall and forms a lush carpet of saw-toothed leaves. It requires an acid soil rich in humus and thrives in dense or light shade, particularly in woodsy places and under evergreens. Succeeds in all but the very coldest areas.

Ivy geranium (Pelargonium peltatum), about 12'' tall, makes a handsome, year-round ground cover in areas where frosts do not occur. Bonus is its lovely white and pink blossoms. Grows in light sun or shade, prefers light, well-drained soil kept on the dry side.

Creeping rosemary (Rosmarinus officinalis variety) has needle-like leaves and grows to about 24'' or less. A useful ground cover in hot, dry areas; it tolerates seaside conditions. Grows in warmer areas.

Mother-of-thyme or Creeping thyme (Thymus serpyllum) is a pungent-smelling herb that grows 1'' to 6'' tall and bears tiny, purple flowers. Good in rock gardens and rocky locations, it is often used between stepping stones. Needs sun and dry, well-drained soil.

Vinca minor—periwinkle and creeping myrtle are other names for it —has beautiful, blue flowers in spring, spreads a dark-green carpet of shiny leaves that chokes out grass and weeds. Good in light or deep shade, in deep, rich, moist soil on the acid side.

Mulches, Another Kind of Ground Cover

Mulch is the paydirt of the garden, providing a rich harvest while enriching the soil for the crops that will follow. Mulch is nothing new; nature has been creating it ever since the first leaves fell to the ground. For that's what mulch is—a ground covering. The springy carpet on a forest floor is a natural example.

The forest carpet decomposes, adding nutrients to the soil below. An organic garden mulch does the same thing, while at the same time adding humus to the soil and improving its structure. Man simply takes his cue from nature, applying his own ground covering, natural or inorganic.

Mulching reduces or eliminates one of the gardener's most onerous chores—weeding—by depriving these pesky plants of the sunlight they need for growth. The isolated weed that does poke through is easily dispatched. In part, this easy weeding is a result of another benefit: moisture retention. Mulch slows moisture evaporation, protecting tender new roots from overheated soil while also lessening the watering chore.

A mulch can consist of inorganic materials such as gravel and stones (sometimes used around trees and in flower beds) or organic coverings such as manure or even ground corncobs. The latter, of course, is not one of the most readily available materials and availability is one factor in selecting a mulch.

Ground bark. Inexpensive, attractive, long lasting. Available chip-sized or finely ground.

Peat moss. Expensive and somewhat difficult to prepare. Initially attractive but can dry out, lose esthetic appeal, and shed water, as from a duck's back.

Pine needles. Durable, resist disturbance by wind. Good mulch for strawberries. Potential fire hazard when dry.

Grass clippings. Probably the most available mulch to the average gardener. Mats quickly, generating heat and disagreeable results if initial application is too thick. Spread thinly, allow to dry before applying to garden.

Straw. One of the best mulch choices. Long lasting, can reduce moisture evaporation by as much as 70%. Will deplete soil nitrogen which should be replaced by adding nitrogen fertilizer or bloodmeal.

Sawdust. A good choice, easily obtainable in many areas. Easy to handle but can rob nitrogen from soil; replenish nitrogen as with straw.

Plastic film. Black, polyethylene film is an excellent mulch, but unattractive where esthetics are a consideration. (Of course, it can be covered with ground bark, either chip-sized or finely ground.) Keeps soil temperature even, eliminates weeds entirely. Punch holes for water penetration.

Newspaper. Readily available, builds humus. Can be used shredded or in sheets to desired thickness. Can be held in place by rocks, bricks, or soil and can be covered for better appearance. Ink actually contains trace materials beneficial to plant growth.

Each gardener has his or her own favorite mulch or mulches, depending on personal preference and special requirements. One gardener, Ruth Stout, sister of mystery writer Rex Stout, was so enthusiastic about the advantages of mulching that she wrote a bestselling book about it, *How To Have a Green Thumb Without an Aching Back*. It probably can be said without contradiction that there are few people who would be inspired enough by mulching to write a book about it, but most who try mulching will sing its praises.

7•Home-Grown Vegetables are the Best

Today's commercial tomato is all it takes to make anyone want to plant a vegetable garden. Judging by the results I see in the supermarket and even at many roadside stands, some plant breeder with jaded tastebuds is indeed about to "perfect" the shipping tomato—a tasteless piece of vegetable matter, anemic in color and no longer curvaceous, but square, so that no space is wasted in the carton.

Enough said. If you want to plant a vegetable garden, the ideal spot is slightly sloped in full sun. Soil should be fertile, deep, and well drained, away from trees and shrubs that would give unwanted shade and root competition. Fertility may be improved by the addition of an all-purpose commercial fertilizer, compost, or well-rotted manure which should be added at the time of plowing, tilling, or spading, a little while before the garden is to be planted.

Some provision needs to be made for watering. A good rule of thumb is that vegetables need the equivalent of 1'' of rain each week. An occasional thorough soaking, using perforated hose, is better than frequent sprinkling.

Choice of vegetables for the home garden depends on individual tastes and space available. Easy-to-raise vegetables include lettuce, spinach, tomatoes, radishes, onions, peas, beans, cucumbers, squash, sweet corn, cabbage, carrots, peppers, sometimes okra and eggplant. A plot 24' by 24' or the equivalent is sufficient for four persons, especially with succession croppings (like radishes followed by spinach).

First, plan your garden on paper, giving thought to space and light needed for various crops. Beans, peas, corn, okra, radishes, beets, and carrots are typical row crops; leaf lettuce and spinach are sometimes grown in beds; cucumbers, squash, pumpkin, and melons are grown in hills; hybrid tomatoes are staked upright. Be careful to keep one crop from shading another and to keep vines from overrunning another crop's space. Climbers such as pole beans can utilize a fence.

If your space in the sun is very limited, you can plant a salad garden in as little as 50 square feet. There can be surprising beauty and productivity in such a garden. For example, the color, shape, and formation of different loose-leaf and head lettuces, along with green onions, curly parsley, radishes, spinach, purple-leaved Dark Opal basil, and maybe a few plants of brilliant red rhubarb chard. Beauty is also a crop, so plan this garden

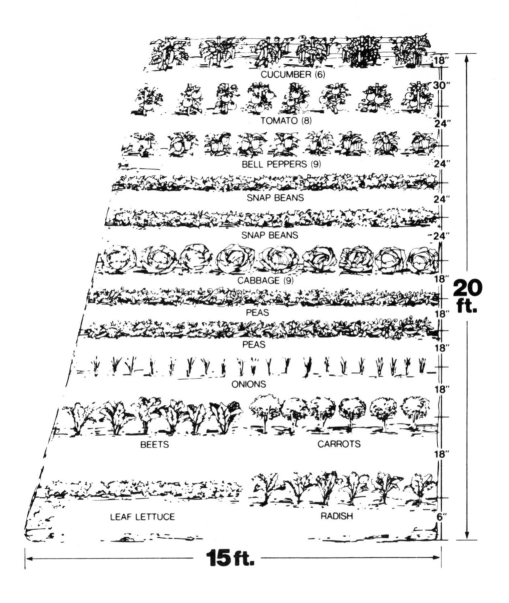

CUCUMBER (6)

18"
30"

TOMATO (8)

24"

BELL PEPPERS (9)

24"

SNAP BEANS

24"

SNAP BEANS

24"

CABBAGE (9)

18"

PEAS

18"

PEAS

18"

ONIONS

18"

BEETS   CARROTS

18"

LEAF LETTUCE   RADISH

6"

20 ft.

15 ft.

A plan for a 15' x 20' vegetable garden.

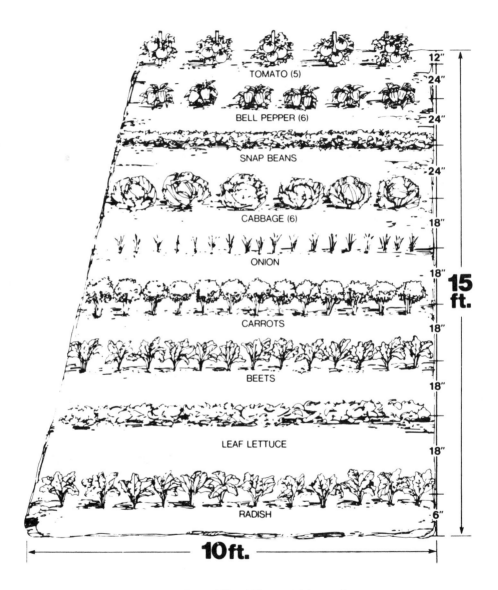

A plan for a 10' x 15' vegetable garden.

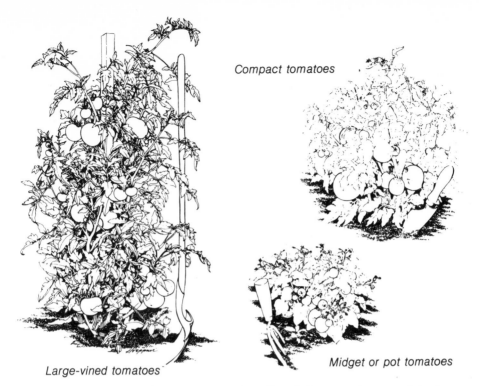

Compact tomatoes

Large-vined tomatoes

Midget or pot tomatoes

carefully on paper to juxtapose contrasting foliage colors and textures. Plant in curved rows instead of straight lines, or scatter beds of any single vegetable randomly throughout the plot.

Tomatoes are by and large the most popular vegetable crop. Staking and pruning increase yield and improve quality. Some varieties that do well staked, and produce quality fruit, include Big Boy, Rutgers, Moreton Hybrid, and Supersonic. Six-foot 2' x 2's make adequate stakes; soft cloth or special fasteners from your garden center may be used for ties. Set the stakes before planting to avoid root injury. Also, tomato plants can be trained into decorative espalier designs against fences.

As tomato plants grow, pinch out most of the suckers that appear along main stems in the crotches made by leaves against the stem. (Bloom stems grow on the main stem between leaves.) Sometimes two leaves of a sucker are left to make food for the plant, which is carried up the stem to the fruit.

Not all tomato flower buds grow into ripe fruit. Poor early pollination and cool temperatures, with natural brittleness in blossom stems, may cause blooms to fall off. This problem can be solved by spraying with chemical blossom-set (dilute naphthoxyacetic acid) to fully-opened blooms.

If your vegetable garden is restricted to a high-rise terrace or an apartment window sill, there are some vegetables you can grow, provided the space receives several hours of full sun and there is enough room to use pots at least 8'' in diameter. To be successful you will have to water often enough so that soil in the pots is never severely dry, and feed with a liquid fertilizer once every two weeks. Cherry tomatoes do especially well in containers, but now there are larger-size hybrids available, bred especially for container culture. Depending on space, you can also grow leaf lettuce, beet greens, spinach, green onions, cucumbers, chard—almost any vegetable, in fact, but especially the midget or dwarf types listed in most large seed catalogs.

VEGETABLE PLANTING AND HARVESTING CHART

Cold-hardy plants for early spring planting
(numbers in parentheses indicate days from planting until harvest)

Very hardy [plant 4 to 6 weeks before frost-free date]

Broccoli (70-150)   Peas (58-75)
Cabbage (65-110)   Potato (90-120)
Lettuce (45-50)   Spinach (35-45)
Onions (90-130)   Turnips (42-55)

Hardy [plant 2 to 4 weeks before frost-free date]

Beets (55-80)   Mustard (45-60)
Carrots (60-85)   Parsnips (110-130)
Chard (45-55)   Radish (23-30)

Bush green or wax beans

Bush limas or "butterbeans"

Acorn squash at various stages of maturity

Cold-tender or heat-hardy plants for late spring or early summer planting

Not cold-hardy [plant on frost-free date]

Beans, snap (45-72)
Corn, sweet (65-90)
Okra (55-60)

Squash (50-60)
Tomato (65-90)

Requiring hot weather [plant 1 week or more after frost-free date]

Beans, lima (65-78)
Cucumber (55-75)
Eggplant (70-85)

Melons (80-95)
Peppers (62-80)
Sweet potato (120-150)

Medium heat-tolerant [good for summer planting]

Beans, all (45-72)
Chard (45-55)

Corn, sweet (65-90)
Squash (50-60)

Hardy plants for late summer or fall planting except in the North
[plant 6 to 8 weeks before first fall freeze]

Beets (55-60)
Collards (70-80)
Kale (55-70)
Lettuce (45-76)

Mustard (45-60)
Spinach (35-45)
Turnips (42-55)

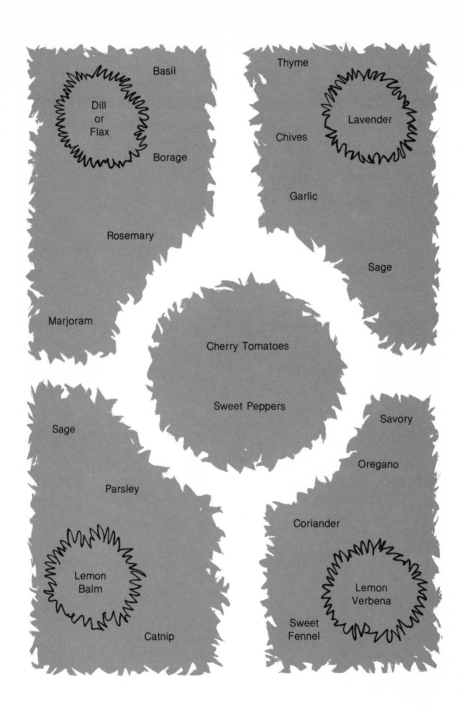

Plan for an herb garden

8•Herbs—Ancient Traditions, Modern Delights

Through the centuries man has utilized plants as real or imagined cures for his ailments. The Greeks used dried crocus stigmas as an eye balm. The Romans reveled in the rose as a hangover cure. And just about everyone utilized nature's authentic medicine plants: herbs. Apothecaries devoted their lives to studying the medicinal properties of herbs. Entire gardens, often arranged in elaborate geometric patterns, were devoted to these wonderflora.

The use of herbs as a base for modern drugs proves the wisdom of at least some of the ancients. The herbs' best known place in the modern scene, however, is the kitchen, where they add a dash of elegance to the plainest of dishes and earn a heady measure of appreciation for the cook.

Since herbs are as delightful to grow as they are to use, you can easily double your cooking laurels and triple your fun by becoming a gourmet gardener—without leaving the kitchen. One of the numerous plusses of these remarkable plants is their versatility. Many can be grown indoors as well as out, lending their utilitarian beauty to a sunny window sill. Or, if you want, you can emulate our Colonial cousins and plant a dooryard herb garden.

Herbs, for all their delicate flavor, are hearty, easy-to-grow plants. There are books and even societies devoted to herbs, but all you need to get growing are a few fundamentals. Just remember, they like ''dry feet and warm heads.'' Most herbs do require regular watering, but they should not be left standing in it. Although sun is a basic need for most herbs, there are a few, such as parsley and mint, that do well in light shade.

Although herbs generally prefer a soil that is slightly alkaline, they are remarkably lenient when it comes to putting down roots. In fact, if the soil is too rich, they will spend their energy producing large leaves, neglecting their true purpose in your life—fragrance and flavor. Herbs aren't fussy about soil composition, but they do like it light if possible; it should be friable and spaded to a depth of from 6'' to 10'' to permit easy water penetration and root growth.

Like their vegetable and flower cousins, herbs are either classified as annuals (life cycle completed in a single year) or perennials (plants that live from year to year). Unlike most of their cousins, many herbs grow more compactly as a result of harvest pruning, making possible neat, limited-space plantings. The intricate knot gardens of Colonial days were also made possible by this hedge-like ornamental habit.

Another modern convenience, one also rooted in the past, is a kitchen herb garden. Try herbs in planters on a sunny kitchen windowsill for finger-tip convenience. Hanging planters is another possibility. Or grow them under two 20-, 30-, or 40-watt fluorescent tubes burned 16 hours out of every 24; place them so that the tops of the plants are about 4'' directly under the tubes.

The optimal time to harvest, indoors or out, is when the plant oils are highest—during the sunny morning hours. Tender leaves can be cut as soon as the plants are well established. On flowering varieties, the harbinger of harvest are the blossoms—cut and gather just as they begin to open. Blooms and leaves are harvested together on flowering herbs, a simple task of clipping off the tops.

Herbs, whether annual or perennial, have two lives, both equally delightful. The first is when they lend their fresh, spicy essence to summertime meals. The second begins when that essence is captured in dried leaves and flowers and carefully stored. A bottle genie couldn't add a finer touch of magic to the aromas of a wintertime kitchen.

Preparation of herbs for their second life is simple. Dry the cuttings by spreading them on a flat surface that will permit free circulation of air. A window screen works well. When the leaves are dry (crisp) strip them from the stems and store in airtight bottles. Then wait until just before you are ready to use them before crushing the required amount.

Another cooking convenience, and one many people are unaware of, is that some herbs freeze readily. I found these suggestions in the seed catalog of the Jackson & Perkins Company: "Harvest and wash the leaves of dill, chives, tarragon, and basil in the same manner as for drying, but leave the foliage on the stem. Bunch and tie; using the string for dipping, blanch them in unsalted boiling water for 50 seconds. Then cool them in ice water for a few minutes. Remove the leaves from their stems, wrap the leaves in freezer bags or foil and place in the freezer."

Ten Great Herbs

Sweet basil. Annual, 1' to 2' tall. Leaves green or purple. Tiny, white flowers. Use as walkway border; can be potted for patio or terrace gardens. Repels flies and mosquitoes. Sow seeds after last frost. Pinch stems to promote bushier growth. Gather leaves before bloom. Basil has a slight peppery taste. Use for salads, vinegars, sauces, vegetable dishes (especially freshly-sliced tomatoes), and stuffings. Basil is also easy to grow as a house plant, either in a sunny, warm window or fluorescent-light garden.

Chive. Perennial, 2' tall, grass-like clumps. Tubular leaves, pompon-shaped lavender flowers. Has mild, onion flavor. Use in salads, soups, omelets, souffles, baked potatoes. Chive clumps make excellent ornamentals anywhere in the landscape. Chive planted near carrots is said to improve their growth and flavor. One of the easiest, most useful herbs to grow in a kitchen herb garden. Chive is evergreen in mild climates. Likes

Sweet Basil   Chives   Dill

sun, moist soil. Divide clumps and pot for indoor use during winter; they'll grow best, however, if allowed to be frosted for a few weeks, then brought inside.

Dill. Annual, 3' to 4' tall. Lacy, light-green leaves. Dill leaves add delicate flavor to meat dishes (notably lamb), salads, fish. Seeds have slightly bitter taste that enhances sauces, homemade breads. Stems and seeds are widely used in pickling. Dill makes a nice background for the flower garden. Delicate edging on walkways. Companion to cabbage, improves health and growth. Sow dill seeds. Repeat sowings for summer-long supply. Start clipping a few leaves when the plants are 6' tall. Harvest seeds when ripe, brown, and flat.

Sweet marjoram. Perennial (in mild climates), 1' to 2' tall. Tiny, gray-green leaves. Bushy plant, purplish-pink flowers. A sweet, spicy herb. Complements sauteed or stuffed mushrooms, salads, vinegars,

Sweet Marjoram   Mint   Oregano

meats, sauces, wine marinades. Attractive in containers and as a border plant for walkways or flower beds. Plant throughout the garden if you like, for sweet marjoram is said to add flavor to vegetables. Sow seeds or grow from cuttings or root divisions. Prefers sun, moist soil. In cold climates, bring inside for winter.

Mint. Perennial, 1' to 3' tall. Spearmint, peppermint, orange mint, golden apple mint—all four varieties have purplish flowers. Leaf color ranges from dark green to green streaked with purple and yellow. Use mint for garnishes. Crushed leaves add zing to cole slaw, vegetables, and make great teas. Add to sauces for refreshing taste for lamb or veal. Garnish for fruit desserts and lemonade. Use mint as an aromatic plant that can add a touch of freshness to your home. Improves the condition of tomatoes; deters cabbage moth when planted nearby. Start mint from seeds or cuttings. Likes sun or shade. Cut flowering stalks before they go to seed. The more frequently cut, the better mints grow; they do need fairly rich, moist soil.

Oregano. Perennial, about 2½' tall. Oval, green leaves, medium size. Purplish-pink flowers, spreading habit. This pungent relative of sweet marjoram may be used fresh or dried on meat and vegetable dishes, salads and sauces (especially tomato). Sometimes called the "pizza herb." Oregano does well in containers. Its habit also makes it useful as a ground cover for banks. Grow oregano from divisions or seeds. Likes sun, moderate amounts of water. Pick leaves as needed.

Parsley. Biennial. Finely curled, triple curled, or plain. Grows 6" to 12" tall. Glossy, dark-green leaves. Refreshing pungence. Use as a garnish on salads, meats, seafood; use for dressings with vegetables. Widely used as a garnish and in bouquets for flavoring stews, sauces. Good as seasoner, alone, and with chives and onions. Parsley makes an attractive edging for walks or flower beds. Decorative indoor plant. Sow parsley seeds after soaking overnight in water, or transplant potted plants. Prefers partial shade. Pick leaves from mature plants before the flowers appear.

Rosemary. Perennial, 4' to 6' tall. Gray-green foliage, pale-blue flowers. Not dependably winter hardy in cold-winter climates; bring inside before freezing. A fragrant mint, often used in stuffings. Sprinkle on chick-

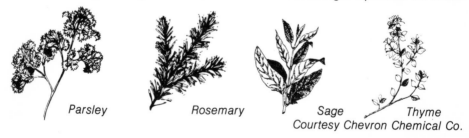

Parsley   Rosemary   Sage   Thyme
Courtesy Chevron Chemical Co.

en, lamb and roasts for a spicy flavor. Rosemary can be trained as a hedge. The prostrate form makes an excellent ground cover. Rosemary keeps away bean beetles, cabbage moths, and carrot flies. Plant started seedlings or sow seeds that have been soaked overnight in water. Likes a dry, sunny spot. Give young plants a frequent tip pinching to direct growth.

Sage. Perennial, up to 2' tall. Shrub-like. Gray-green, oblong leaves. Sage is a slightly bitter herb. Excellent in stuffings, especially in chicken, turkey, and baked fish. Great in herb bread. Makes a stately, low hedge around gardens or walkways. Repels cabbage moth and carrot fly. Start sage from seed or cuttings. Sow indoors at first, then transplant. Cut back to encourage growth.

Thyme. Perennial, a shrub-like plant that grows 8'' to 12'' tall. Loose pink or lilac flowers on both varieties. Thyme gives a clove-like flavor that enhances stews, gumbos, chowders, and cooked vegetables. Add to sauces for turkey and fish. Thyme makes an excellent ground cover. Shrub varieties may be potted in containers and grown indoors. Repels cabbage worms. Sow thyme seeds indoors or start from rooted divisions. Dry soil and lots of sun. Thin plants 8'' to 12'' apart. Clip tops when in full bloom.

9•High-Yield Fruit Trees

Fruit trees need full sunlight for best production. Inadequate sunlight delays the beginning of fruit bearing and may reduce the amount of fruit. Avoid placing fruit trees where they will be shaded by buildings or by other trees.

Your trees will grow more vigorously and bear better if they have adequate space to develop their root systems. Do not plant them where roots of forest or shade trees will compete with them for the same soil. To reduce competition from weeds or grass, cultivate and mulch.

Prune young apple trees to develop a strong framework with a central leader and horizontal branches. Excessive upright growth will delay fruit bearing and reduce the quantity of fruit produced.

Your fruit trees normally will begin to bear fruit soon after they have become old enough to blossom freely. Nevertheless, the health of your trees and their environment, their fruiting habits, and the cultural practices you use can influence their ability to produce fruit. Adequate pollination is also essential to fruit yield.

If just one of these conditions is unfavorable, yields may be reduced. Perhaps the tree will not bear fruit at all. As a grower, you can exercise some control over most of the factors contributing to fruit production.

Bearing Age

When you purchase nursery-grown fruit trees, their tops will probably be from one to two years old. The length of time from planting to fruit bearing varies with the type of fruit. Trees that grow at a moderate rate generally bear fruit sooner than those that grow either too quickly or too slowly.

The ages (from planting) when trees can be expected to bear fruit are as follows:

Apple	2-5
Apricot	2-5
Cherry, sour	3-5
Cherry, sweet	4-7
Citrus	3-5
Fig	2-3
Peach	2-4
Pear	4-6
Plum	3-6
Quince	5-6

A vest-pocket orchard for a typical suburban lot. *Three levels are accommodated in this miniature orchard at the rear of a small, suburban lot. The three tiers are separated by rock-held retaining walls. 1. Espaliered pyracantha or euonymus. 2. Upright yew, weeping peach or dwarf fruiting peach. 3. A bed of floribunda roses. 4. Pink dogwood, pink wisteria or flowering or fruiting peach. 5. Ivy or euonymus. 6. Blue spruce or cutleaf birch. 7. Border of early spring bulbs followed by annuals for late summer and fall bloom, including cactus dahlias and Gloriosa daisies. 8. Crimson King maple, mountain ash or Rubylace locust. 9. Lilac or redbud. 10. Clump birch. 11. Andorra juniper. 12. A lightly shaded garden of azaleas, lilies and caladiums. 13. Austrian pine, Norway spruce or Russian olive trees. 14. Japanese pagoda tree or pin oak shade tree. 15. Blueberry bushes, Nanking cherry bushes. 16. Blackberries and dewberries staked to fencing. 17. Raspberries on supports. 18. Dwarf apricot and nectarines, pear and peach trees. 19. Asparagus bed. 20. Celery planting. 21. Rhubarb clumps. 22. Currants and/or serviceberries. 23. Small garden of salad makings and melons. 24. Gooseberries. 25. Grapes staked. 26. June and everbearing strawberries. 27.*

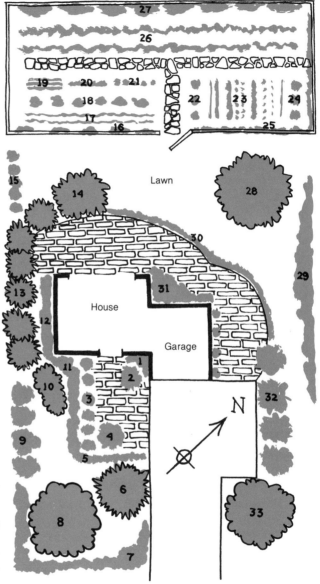

Dwarf apple, cherry or apricot trees along here; some may be espaliered on fence. 28. Weeping willow, ginkgo or sycamore tree. 29. Perennial bed including early bulbs and chrysanthemums for fall. 30. Edging of Japgarden juniper. 31. Perennial herb garden, basil, thyme, others. 32. Lilac, crape-myrtle, tamarix, or althea. 33. Redbud or weeping or fruiting peach.

Dwarf apple and dwarf pear trees usually begin to bear one to two years earlier than standard-size trees.

Tree Health

Healthy trees produce good-quality fruit. Weak or diseased trees produce fruit of poor quality or no fruit at all. The first step in fruit production is to keep your fruit trees healthy.

Two of the main problems involved are insects and diseases. Typical of diseases that attack and destroy leaves and young fruit on apple and pear trees is scab fungus, which causes the brown rot that kills blossoms on peach trees and plum trees.

Diseases, insects, and fungi can be controlled through application of spray mixtures recommended by your county agricultural agent or state experiment station. These spray mixtures of fungicides and insecticides are usually effective against most fruit-tree pests. When fruit trees are not sprayed properly or left untreated, diseases and insects may restrict the size and quality of the yield, although the trees themselves usually continue to bear fruit.

Climate and Weather

Most hardy fruit trees need a certain amount of cold winter weather to end their dormancy and to promote spring growth. When winters are too mild, spring growth is delayed, irregular, and slow. These factors extend the period of blooming, and thereby increase the possibility of frost injury.

Hardy fruit trees grown in climates considerably warmer than their native ones often bear poorly because of insufficient winter cold. This problem can occur in areas with mild climates such as Southern California and within 200 miles of the Gulf of Mexico.

On the other hand, extreme cold during winter dormancy may kill the fruit buds. Winter weather rarely threatens hardy apple, pear, plum, and sour cherry varieties. Sweet cherry trees, however, are relatively sensitive to cold until they become dormant. Peach trees are very vulnerable to cold weather. Their buds can be killed by midwinter temperatures around -10°F.

As the fruit buds grow and open, they become more susceptible to injury from frost. The exposed buds can usually withstand temperatures near 24°F. However, the open blossoms of practically all fruit trees may be killed if the temperature drops below 27°F.

When a heavy frost is expected, covering the trees will sometimes prevent bud or blossom injury, provided temperatures do not fall too low and the cold weather is of short duration. Protective covering may be effective, and such things as cheese cloth and old bed sheets may be used.

During spring frosts, some commercial growers heat their orchards, but this method is impractical for most home gardeners. After a severe frost, injured blossoms may appear normal, but if the pistils (center part of the blossoms) are killed, the tree will not bear fruit that season.

Pollination

Most fruit trees need to be pollinated. Without sufficient pollination they may blossom abundantly, but will not bear fruit.

Some species of fruit trees have perfect flowers, meaning that both the anthers, which contain pollen, and the pistils, which develop into fruit, are located in the same blossom. Trees that bear fruit through self-pollination, or set fruit without pollination, are called "self-fruitful."

However, there are many types of fruit with perfect flowers that cannot produce fruit from their own pollen. These require pollen from another variety and are called "self-unfruitful."

Some species of fruit trees do not fit conveniently into either category. Persimmons and dates have male trees that produce pollen and female trees that produce fruit. To grow them successfully, it is necessary to plant at least one tree of each gender near each other.

Almost all citrus trees are self-fruitful. Other self-fruitful types include quinces, sour cherries, apricots (exceptions are Perfection and Riland), figs (except the Smyrna type grown in California), peaches (except the J.H. Hale and several others), and European-type plums such as the Stanley, Green Gage, and Italian Prune.

Self-unfruitful types include most apple, pear, sweet cherry, and Japanese and American plum trees. To pollinate adequately, plant two or more varieties near each other. Bees and other insects normally pollinate fruit trees. To insure an adequate supply of bees, furnish each acre with at least one colony. However, in small orchards surrounded by uncultivated land, enough resident pollinators may be present. The following planting practices are recommended:

Apple. Plant at least two varieties of apple trees near one another. Golden Delicious, a self-fruitful type, is one of the few exceptions to this rule. Poor pollen-producing types, such as Baldwin, Gravenstein, Staymen, Winesap, and Rhode Island Greening, need to be planted with at least two other varieties to insure adequate pollination of all.

Sweet cherry. Bing, Lambert, and Napoleon (Royal Ann) cherry trees do not pollinate one another. Plant a pollinating variety such as Black

Tartarian, Republican, Van, or Windsor, or a sour cherry, such as Montmorency, nearby.

Pear. Many varieties of pears are completely or partially self-unfruitful. For adequate pollination, plant at least two varieties together. Note: Bartlett and Seckel pears will not pollinate each other, and Magness cannot be used as a pollinator.

Plum. Since most varieties of Japanese and American plums are self-unfruitful, plant two or more varieties together.

Biennial Bearing

Occasionally, certain fruit trees, such as apples, bear heavily one year and sparsely the next. This is called "biennial bearing." The spring-flowering buds of most hardy fruit trees have actually been formed during the previous summer. Therefore, an especially heavy crop one year may prevent adequate bud formation for the following year.

Biennial bearing of apples is difficult to alter or correct. However, you can induce a return to normal yearly fruit production by early and heavy thinning during the year in which the trees are producing their large yield. About 30 to 40 healthy leaves are needed to produce good quality fruit. Within 30 days after bloom, thin to leave only five to 10 fruit per yard along the branches.

10•Berries and Grapes

Although strawberries are probably the most easily grown of all fruits—and the most adaptable in terms of landscape uses—numerous other so-called small fruits, the types that grow on bushes or brambles (blueberries and raspberries, for example) or vines (grapes) are also more readily handled in a home garden than the tree-types such as apple and peach.

Since strawberries are so widely cultivated—both in the ground and in patio containers—I have prepared a series of questions typically asked about them—with the answers:

When should strawberries be planted?

In most areas, spring planting is done as early as the soil can be worked. If the climate is mild, fall planting is recommended, and a fair crop can be expected the following spring. Set the plants with the roots spread out and the crowns slightly above the ground line. Pack the dirt firmly around the roots so that the crown is level with the ground. If planting is done in rows, place the plants 1' to 2' apart in rows 2' to 4' apart.

Should more than one variety be planted?

The wise gardener will plant more than one kind and let taste and climate weed out the better from the best. Ideally, the variety selection would include early, midseason, late, and everbearing varieties. The term "everbearing" is a misnomer, for no strawberry is actually everbearing. Normally strawberries flower in the spring and the fruit ripens in May and June. Through constant selection and breeding, hybridizers have isolated plants that flowered and fruited latest and called these "everbearing."

When and how much fertilizer should be applied?

Prepare the soil for strawberries thoroughly, like you would for a new rose bed. Spade in lots of well-rotted manure—probably twice as much as you'd like to pay for. A commercial fertilizer with an analysis of 10-10-10 (equal parts nitrogen, phosphorus, and potash) is beneficial to keep the plants in good growth. Applied at the rate of 1 pound to 100 square feet, it should cause no burning. Pale-colored foliage indicates a need for nitrogen; dark-green foliage indicates an adequate supply. Too much leaf growth cuts down fruit production. If you test the soil, it should have a pH of 5.5 to 6.5. The texture of the soil is not as important as its content of organic and mineral fertilizers. Dehydrated manures should be spaded into the soil five or 10 days before planting to avoid burning the plants.

Should the "runners" be kept cut from mother plants?

If runners are cut off before they root, the original plants will form "hills." These plants produce the largest, finest berries, but usually the smallest quantity. If the runners are allowed to form and root down at random, a "matted" row results. This culture produces the largest quantity of berries, but also the smallest in size. The strongest two or three runners may be kept on each plant and rooted down in rows on each side of the mother plants. This culture produces an average amount of berries of intermediate size.

Must I put out new plants every year?

Because the strawberry is actually a biennial, the mother plant should be destroyed as soon as it has finished fruiting. If you want to propagate your own plants, take the cut-off runners to a separate bed and grow them for spring planting the next year. If the runners are rooted beside the mother plants, the old plants can be pulled out and the new ones left to produce next year's fruit. However, it is best to completely redo the bed every two years—applying well-rotted manure and spading deeply. If a straw mulch is applied each fall and allowed to decompose into the soil during the following season, this will tend to lessen the need of bi-annual refurbishing.

Are pests a problem with strawberries?

For most home growers the pest problem is negligible, especially if new plants have been purchased. The ideal practice is to put out fresh stock each year, so that there will always be a new crop of freshly set-out plants that will not bloom until next year, and a current bearing crop, which will be destroyed after fruiting.

Is winter mulching necessary?

They will go through the winter in the South without protection. Where alternate hard freezing and thawing occur throughout the fall and winter, wheat, rye, or barley straw makes the best winter mulch. It should be spread 3" or 4" deep before severe freezing weather (20°F or lower) is expected. When the leaves start to grow in the spring, pull the straw from the crowns of the plants and work it into the rows between. It will conserve moisture and keep down weeds. Add new straw if there is not enough left to keep the fruit from getting mud-spattered.

Does the name "strawberry" come from the use of a straw mulch?

No. London boys used to stick a few of the berries on the end of straws while they peddled them in the streets. In Saxon times the plant was called "streouberrie," meaning a berry scattered, which is exactly what strawberry runners will do if they are not clipped back.

Are strawberries actually related to the common garden rose?

Yes. The rose family has flowers with five petals and stamens in a ring around the edge of a sunken cup. The native strawberries that were found from Chile to Oregon were very fragrant. Hybridizers have changed the family perfume into one of the most delicious flavors known to the world. Other close relatives of the strawberry include apples, quinces, plums, peaches, raspberries, blackberries, spireas, and geums.

Birds eat my strawberries as fast as they ripen. What can be done?

Mosquito netting can be spread over the beds, unless you can devise some better means of scaring the birds away.

Is it possible to grow strawberries as container plants?

Yes, in pots, tubs, large plastic-lined fruit baskets, and even in hanging containers. Although any variety of strawberry may be planted in a container, the runnerless fraises des bois types are ideal. Allow one 6'' standard pot or its equivalent for each plant. Use a rich potting mixture, for example two parts all-purpose potting soil and two parts sphagnum peat moss to one part each of vermiculite, sand, and bloodmeal. Place containers where the plants will receive at least a half day or more of direct sun; water often enough to keep the soil always moist, never dry.

Bramble Fruits

Raspberries and blackberries can be grown in almost any type of soil, but for best results, a good, well-drained loam, clay loam, or sandy loam soil high in organic matter is recommended. Do not plant in the same soils on which tomatoes, Irish potatoes, peppers, or eggplants have been grown for several successive years. Be certain to order only plants certified to be virus free.

Land preparation. Incorporating a heavy application of stable manure —two bushels per 100 square feet—or a good, green manure crop prior to planting the brambles is beneficial. The soil pH should be 5.5 to 6.0. Spade the soil to a depth of 8'' and rake to provide good tilth for proper planting.

Plant spacing. Red and black raspberries should be planted 2' to 3' apart in the row, whereas Thornfree, Black Satin, and Dirksen blackberries should be spaced 8' apart in the row. The spacing between the rows will depend on the type of cultivating equipment that is available; 4' is normally the best spacing for gardens.

Setting. A hole should be dug sufficiently deep for each plant so that 3'' or 4'' of soil cover the roots. The handle or old cane should be cut off at ground level after a new shoot has developed.

Cultivation. The soil should not be allowed to become too compact. Cultivating 1'' to 2'' deep will control weeds and also increase the oxygen exchange to the roots. Incorporating organic matter into the soil will reduce the need for cultivation and also improve plant growth. A 3'' to 4'' layer of wood chips—obtained from the tree pruning division of your electric company—will replace the need for all hoeing and cultivation. As the wood chips decay, they will have to be replaced to maintain weed control. Do not use sawdust or pine shavings.

Fertilization. For good bramble production the soil should contain a medium level of phosphorus, potassium, and magnesium; a pH of 5.5 to 6.0 and a boron level of two pounds per acre. On good silt loam, clay loam, or even clay garden soils, the above-mentioned nutrients normally should be applied before planting and repeat applications made about every three years. Nitrogen should be applied every year. Stable manure is an ideal source of nitrogen and potassium. About two bushels per 100 square feet each spring should be ideal. If manure is not available, broadcast one pound of 10-10-10 along each side of the row for every 100' of row. Contact your local Agricultural Extension Service for an insect-control program. One spray at the proper time usually takes care of the problem.

Training. Black raspberries should have the tip of the new cane pinched or cut off at 15'' in height the first year and 22'' to 24'' the second year and subsequent years. This should be done when the new canes are 18'' to 20'' high the first year and 24'' to 28'' high the second and subsequent years. Pinching causes the side branches—which produce the fruit—to develop and also causes the main cane to be sufficiently strong to be self-supporting.

New canes of red raspberries are not cut back the first growing season. They are, however, cut back shortly before the leaves emerge in the second growing season. The amount of cane that is retained is determined by the support system used since red raspberries are not normally self-supporting. Red raspberries can be self-supporting if several canes are cut off at 30''. These canes are tied together to form hills or clusters of plants about every 3'. The canes should be tied together at the 20'' height and again at 28''. No more than six canes should be tied together. Excess plants should be cut off at ground level. Cutting the plants off at 30'' is easier and less expensive, but in so doing you remove the early maturing fruit as it is produced from buds that occur near the end of the canes.

Thornless blackberries should have their fruit-producing canes tied in the shape of a fan to a wire or wooden trellis in March. The canes should be cut off at the 4' to 6' length. The length will be determined by the cane position on the trellis, number of canes retained, and vigor of the plant. The new canes that will produce next year's fruit should be left on the ground but trained down the row under the existing fruiting canes.

Pruning. Black raspberry fruiting canes may be removed after harvest but it is much easier to wait until the following March. The same procedure is also true for Latham red raspberry and thornless blackberries. Southland red raspberry, however, is an everbearer (it produces a crop of fruit on the tip of the new canes in August, September, and early October and a June crop the following summer on the lower section of the same cane). As a result, the tip of the cane that produced fruit in the fall is removed the following March. The remaining portion of the cane is tied in the manner described under training for red raspberries for the June crop. Those canes can then be removed after harvest or the following March. New canes that emerge in the spring will again provide the fall crop and the following June crop.

Blueberries

Where the climate and soil are suited to blueberries, they not only make wonderful fruiting plants but also fine landscape shrubs. For sure results, plant at least two varieties to insure cross pollination. Varieties such as Bluetta, Berkeley, and Jersey will grow well from coastal New England to North Carolina and west to Michigan and Missouri. Plantings should be located in full sun. Early spring is the best time to plant.

Hybrid highbush blueberries require a uniform supply of moisture. They will not tolerate poorly-drained soil or extremely dry sandy soils. Watering during dry periods will assure good growth and eliminate many of the problems associated with growing blueberries.

Blueberries require a soil pH of 4.0 to 5.5, which is quite acid. The lower pH is better for the high organic, sandy soils and the higher pH for the heavier low organic, clay-type soils. Use of ammonium sulfate at 2 ounces per small plant or 1/4-pound for a large plant will acidify the soil and release the nitrogen needed for proper growth.

How to plant. Soak the roots in water for one hour. Prune off about 1/3 of the top growth. Dig a hole 15'' in diameter and 12'' deep. Mix well-decayed leaves, grass clippings, or peat moss with soil removed from the hole. Place plant into the partially-filled hole and cover roots with soil. Be certain that all roots are covered with 1'' of soil and that the top roots are not more than 2'' below normal ground level. Be certain that the soil is packed firmly about the roots and then water immediately.

Grapes and Other Small Fruits

Grapes, gooseberries, and currants are among the easier fruits to grow in a home garden. Plant hybrid stock in early spring, following directions packed with the stock. For best varieties to plant in your area, contact the Agricultural Extension Service. They will also have recommendations for control of specific insect and disease problems that may occur in your region.

11•House Plants

The therapeutic value of gardening has been recognized for nearly 200 years in Europe, but not until after World War II did the idea begin to catch on, at first in hospitals and other institutions; but now with everyone. In fact, recent psychiatric studies have shown that the more urbanized we become, the greater is the need each and everyone of us has for living plants in our immediate surroundings. And, if you should by chance live or work on the 32nd floor or higher, this need is acute. If you have a fear of flying, it may not be far-fetched to suggest that carrying a small, potted plant with you could help.

Growing plants in pots indoors can get just about as complicated as you want it to be—the same as the pursuit of cooking can lead from the survival basics to gourmet classics. However, the absolute basics for growing plants indoors are really simple. In order for a plant to grow indoors in a pot, here is what it needs:

1. Light: Bright enough to read by, or direct sun.
2. Temperatures comfortable for you.
3. A pleasantly-moist atmosphere, ideally 30% to 60% relative humidity.
4. A growing medium kept suitably moist.
5. Protection from bugs.

Light. All plants need light in order to grow, but not all need direct sun. If you have a place where you want plants and it receives daylight bright enough for you to read or do needlework by, then here are some plants that will grow: Chinese evergreen (Aglaonema), aspidistra (cast-iron plant), prayer plant (Maranta) and its relative, calathea (available in about 25 varieties, most of which have colorful, variegated foliage), sansevieria (snake plant), spider plant (Chlorophytum comosum variety), and almost any of the dracaenas but especially Dracaena fragrans, D. Janet Craig, and D. massangeana.

If you have no natural light strong enough to nurture healthy plants, try using fluorescent light. The standard setup consists of two 20-, 30-, or 40-watt tubes in an industrial fixture that will measure, respectively, 24'', 36'', or 48'' long. Each of these will light a table or shelf up to 24'' wide on which plants will be placed to grow. The tubes should be 3'' to 12'' directly above the plant leaves. Burn the lights 12 to 16 hours out of every 24. Use a combination of one Cool White and one Warm White in each fixture, or use special agricultural-growth fluorescents such as Naturescent, Vita-Lite, Gro-Lux Wide Spectrum, or Verilux TruBloom.

Temperature. Although there are plants that can't be grown in average house or office temperature ranges, most of the varieties commonly distributed can. In other words, daytime temperatures can vary between 65° and 80°F, with a drop at night to somewhere between 60° and 70°F. What is also important is to protect plants from either very cold or very hot drafts of air.

Humidity. During the winter heating season, many houses and offices have less than 10% relative humidity. This isn't enough for the best plant growth (and probably not for your own health, either). You can raise humidity around plants by placing the pots on trays kept filled with pebbles and water, but to be really effective, it is much better to use a cool-vapor humidifier during the winter heating season. This can be a portable unit or room- or small-house-size, or installed as a part of the heating system. Misting the leaves with water helps raise the humidity, but only briefly. Misting is a good habit to get into, however, because it replaces the rain that the same plants you are growing would enjoy in nature.

Soil and water. You can grow most house plants in pre-mixed packages, which may be labeled as all-purpose, for cacti or succulents, or for African violets. In practice, growers use countless recipes for attaining maximum success with a given plant. However, these recipes have served me well over the years and if you don't have favorites of your own, I recommend them:

All-Purpose Potting Mix: Mix together two parts of garden soil to two parts sphagnum peat moss and one part sand (or perlite).

Cacti and Other Succulents Potting Mix: Mix together two parts sand to one part each of garden soil and sphagnum peat moss.

African Violet Potting Mix: Mix together equal parts garden soil, sphagnum peat moss, vermiculite, and sand (or perlite).

In general, plants growing in either all-purpose or African-violet mix should be watered often enough to keep the growing medium in a range between evenly moist and slightly, repeat *slightly*, on the dry side. Those growing in the cacti and other succulents mix should be maintained in a range between evenly moist and on the dry side, which is to say a little drier than the other kinds of plants, especially in cold or damp weather.

Healthy plants benefit from regular applications of fertilizer, diluted and applied according to directions on the label. There are numerous chemical houseplant fertilizers on the market, as well as organics such as fish emulsion. House plants need little or no fertilizer in fall and early winter.

Bug protection. House plants are commonly attacked by cottony, white mealybugs, brown scale, red spider-mites, aphids, and white flies. Among chemicals, malathion is the control for mealybugs, synthetic pyrethrin (Resmethrin) is most effective for white flies, and a miticide (Kelthane or Dimite, for example) best for red spider-mites. Simply washing the plants in tepid water every few days can also help rid a plant of bugs, especially mealybugs, spider-mites, aphids, and white flies.

Best House Plants for Flowers

If you want to grow house plants that will give some flowers almost every day of the year, these are outstanding:

Aeschynanthus (lipstick vine)
Begonia semperflorens
Crossandra
Hibiscus, Chinese
Impatiens

Oxallis crassipes and O. regnellii
Pelargonium (geranium)
Saintpaulia (African violet)
Sinningia (gloxinia)
Spathiphyllum (peace lily)

Although some of these plants will bloom well in a bright, north-facing window that receives little or no direct sunlight, most of them will give a better show if they receive at least morning or afternoon sun. Or, you can place kinds like African violet and spathiphyllum a few feet back from a sunny, south-facing window, perhaps with cacti and other succulents placed directly on the sill to receive maximum light.

Part 3
Special Gardens for Special Purposes
–and People

What you choose to grow in your garden is a matter of personal taste. If you're fascinated by the elusive fragrance of the freesia, or of creeping thyme when you walk across it, then you will naturally collect pleasingly-scented plants. If you're a birdwatcher, then you'll want lots of berried shrubs, some planted thicket-fashion to provide nesting places.

Essentially, this chapter is a collection of garden ideas for anyone with the collector spirit—or some specialized gardening interest.

Rock Gardens and Dry Walls

If you have a steep bank where grass won't grow, or is too difficult to mow, turn it into a rock garden. If you need any kind of retaining wall on your property, think twice before you construct it without pockets for rock plants. In short, some of the real garden dazzlers do best among rocks, and that's why gardeners with perfectly-level plots bring in mounds of earth so they can create little hills and valleys. Moving in rocks is no easy matter, especially large ones which you mostly want to bury so that only a mysterious outcropping shows above the soil. However, there is a lightweight lava rock available called Featherock which is considerably easier to work with (about 20% the weight of regular stone).

If you have to bring stones to your rock garden, the best way is to select all the same kind, and preferably from your own region. Let surfaces slant back into the earth, and if there is an obvious grain in the rock, keep it all going in the same direction.

Before bringing in plants, prepare pockets for them using a growing medium consisting of equal parts garden loam, sand, and sphagnum peat moss (or well-rotted compost).

Perennial flowers for your rock garden might include these: Achillea tomentosa, Persian candytuft, Aquilegia akitensis, thrift, aubrieta, Campanula carpatica, snow-in-summer cerastium, Cheddar pink, draba, gentian, crane's-bill geranium, Gypsophila repens, sun-rose, dwarf iris, lavender, evening-primrose, penstemon, wood phlox, Saponaria ocymoides (bouncing Bet), sedum, sempervivum, thyme, and Verbena bipannatifida.

Annual flowers that do well in rocky situations include ageratum, globe amaranth, calliopsis, nierembergia, Dahlberg daisy, ice plant, dwarf marigold, periwinkle, pinks, rose-moss, dwarf snapdragons, and sweet-alyssum.

For a dry wall in the sun, try Achillea tomentosa, Aurinia saxatilis (basket-of-gold alyssum), Artemisia frigida, snow-in-summer cerastium, crane's-bill geranium, Gypsophila repens, sun-rose, perennial candytuft,

Plan for rock garden in both sun and shade. *1. Maidenhair fern. 2. Ajuga. 3. Aquilegia akitensis. 4. Astilbe. 5. Campanula carpatica. 6. Dicentra eximia. 7. Heuchera. 8. Primrose. 9. Ageratum. 10. Rose-moss. 11. Sweet-alyssum. 12. Achillea tomentosa. 13. Persian candytuft. 14. Cheddar pink. 15. Dwarf iris. 16. Lavender. 17. Wood phlox.*

Phlox subulata, Ceratostigma plumbaginoides, Nepeta mussini, evening-primrose, sedum, and sempervivum.

For a dry wall facing north or otherwise shaded, select from maiden-hair fern, ajuga, Aquilegia akitensis, astilbe, aubrieta, Campanula carpatica, Delphinium nudicaule, Dicentra eximia, Gentiana septemfida, heuchera, Polemonium reptans, primrose, pulmonaria, sedum, and thalictrum.

In times past, keeping a rock garden weed-free and tidy looking was a big problem, especially around the perimeters where it often joined the lawn. Now there is a solution, the string-line trimmer. Since it has no blades that could be damaged by working too close to a rock, this tool is ideal in this situation, and will enable you to have a fantastic garden in practically all seasons without any hard labor.

To help in planning your rock garden, I have designed one that includes plants for full, hot sun, as well as those that do better in a little shade where the soil is dependably moist. Although I have kept my plant suggestions somewhat limited to the varieties most widely distributed and, presumably, the most dependable in a variety of conditions, any low-growing or trailing plant may be considered as a possibility for a rock garden.

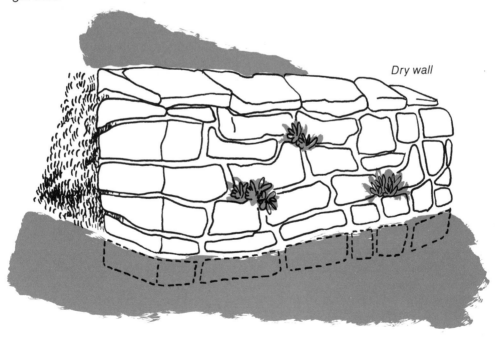

Dry wall

1•Water Gardens—Cooling, Splashing, Reflecting

Fountains, streams, waterfalls, lily pools, birdbaths—contained and directed in countless ways, water is one of the most fascinating details in the landscape.

The only simple and "instant" way to have a splashing fountain or waterfall is to buy a prefabricated unit—and even these require some attention to plumbing. Beyond these examples, check with a local nursery or plumber, or consult large mail-order catalogs such as Sears or Montgomery Ward.

Natural streams, lily pools, and birdbaths or other small basins that hold a little reflecting mirror of water are more easily managed in the home garden.

Easiest water garden of all is a tub—wooden, galvanized, or an old bathtub—sunk in the ground, the edges camouflaged by pieces of relatively flat stone. There are many water plants that do well in a small space. Water-lilies will grow with 4'' of water over the crown, although 8'' is better. Try a combination of Paul Hariot water-lily, water-hyacinth, water-poppies, and Japanese arrowhead. Or Joanne Pring water-lily, water-poppies, blue water-iris, and fish-grass. Mail-order catalogs from water-garden specialists list these and countless other suitable plant materials, plus fish.

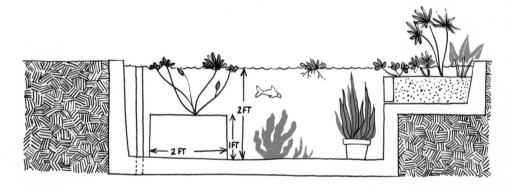

Plan for a pool

2•Nearly-Wild Gardens You Can Grow Almost Anywhere

The free spirit of a wild flower is something that appeals to nearly all of us. One way to have wild flowers is to cultivate them in your own garden. Unless they are growing on your property, it is generally best to buy started plants either locally or by mail from a nursery that knows how to grow wildlings.

Among the best of the wild flowers to bring into your garden are these: bellwort, bloodroot, cardinal flower, columbine, dogtooth violet, Dutchman's-breeches, jack-in-the-pulpit, hepatica, May-apple, rue anemone, Solomon's-seal, spring beauty, violets, Virginia bluebell, wake-robin (trillium), white snakeroot, wild geranium, wild ginger, and woods phlox.

The other approach with wild-flower gardening is to set cultivated flowers free. Here's how this works: You buy packets of cultivated flowers and sow them broadcast-fashion in a meadow, in a sunny spot alongside a stream, or by the roadside. Kinds well suited to this treatment include sweet-alyssum, forget-me-not, calliopsis, bachelor's-button, clarkia, cleome, larkspur, echium, California poppies, Iceland poppies, Shirley poppies, Gilia rubra, godetia, annual baby's-breath helianthus, limnanthes, flax, nicotiana, nigella, mignonette, rudbeckia, and zinnia—a list with almost limitless possibilities.

3•Fragrant Plants and Flowers

Sometimes before we see a flower we are aware of the fragrance. Sweet-olive, for example. Tiny, creamy-white blossoms nestle in the leaves, quite unnoticeable—but the fragrance is something else. Visit New Orleans in almost any season and forever more you will recall the incredible scent of the sweet-olive.

Fragrance gardening has only one rule, and this is common sense. Less is more. Which means, if you plant a garden composed entirely of sweet-smelling flowers and scented leaves, it may be overwhelming.

Fragrant flowers for spring. Trailing arbutus, Daphne cneorum, lily-of-the-valley, lilac, Viburnum carlesi, the honeysuckle known as Lonicera syringantha, certain Darwin and Cottage tulips, Crocus imperati, Leucojum vernum or snowflake, bearded iris, peonies, hyacinths, and daffodils.

Fragrant flowers for summer: Roses, mock-orange, sand-verbena, annual candytuft, pinks and carnations, flowering tobacco (nicotiana), mignonette, lilies, jasmine, gardenia, Clethra alnifolia, butterfly bush, heliotrope, moonflower, lavender, certain petunias, and summer phlox.

Fragrant flowers for autumn: Tuberose, saffron crocus, sweet autumn clematis, chrysanthemums—and those cherished last roses of the season.

Potpourri Captures Summer Scents...

...and releases them for winter pleasure. A well-made potpourri has the amazing ability to stir the subconscious and pique the imagination. Potpourri is indeed the substance of more than fragrant flower petals from your own garden. It is also spices from the East, fixatives such as orris-root and additives such as patchouli, vetiver, or santal. Properly balanced, these conjure all kinds of images in the mind.

There are countless recipes for making potpourri, but to get you started, here is a time-honored one for rose potpourri:

2 quarts fragrant rose petals
1 pint lemon-verbena leaves
1/4 cup rosemary leaves
1 tablespoon grated orange peel
4 tablespoons ground orris-root
4 tablespoons mixed crushed spices
(clove, cinnamon, ginger, nutmeg)
5 drops of vetiver or santal oil

Harvest petals and leaves early in the morning, but after the dew has disappeared. Spread to dry for 10 days on a screen, taut cheesecloth, or newspaper in an airy room. Then you are ready to blend petals and leaves together in recipe quantities by tossing lightly. Blend spices, then mix with petals and leaves. Add drops of oil. Place in airtight container to mellow for about six weeks, after which time you can transfer your potpourri to crystal bottles, rose jars, or other attractive containers. Shake or stir occasionally to increase the scent.

4•Moonflowers for a Midsummer Night's Dream Garden

There are two kinds of flowers that have a special beauty in the nighttime. First are those that release a heady aroma in the evening, and second are those that open at night, or which have colors a pale moonlight becomes. All of these are ideal flowers to include in the surround for your outdoor living area.

For nighttime fragrance, select from these flowers: Daphne cneorum, tuberose, lilac, Viburnum carlesi, hyacinth, mock-orange, carnation, butterfly-bush, clethra, gardenia, jasmine, Madonna lily, mignonette, sweet rocket, flowering tobacco (nicotiana), and night-scented stock.

Night-blooming flowers, all having an ethereal beauty in the moonlight, include these: night-blooming cereus (a form of cactus), cooperia (rain lily), pale yellow and pink daylilies (check catalog descriptions as not all remain open in the evening), hybrid white petunias, Madonna lilies, Formosa lilies, centifolium hybrid lilies, flowering tobacco in white, four-o'-clocks, moonflowers, night jessamine (Cestrum nocturnum), tropical water-lilies, Gladiolus tristis, evening campion (Lychnis alba), bouncing Bet, and evening-primrose.

5•Color-Scheme Gardens

If your house is red brick, passionate pink azaleas won't do a thing for it, or for you. But how about flame azaleas in shades of yellow through apricot and orange? If the structural material is gray stone, pinks and reds will look great, or if you're more inclined to the yellows, they'll be fine, too. These simple examples show the complementary effect flower colors can have on building materials.

Color schemes also tend to unify the appearance of a garden. A riot of color, as they say, is not hard to achieve. You just plant willy-nilly, take good care of the plantings, and pretty soon you'll have a fiesta of bloom. More difficult to achieve, but also prettier to look at, are gardenings with a definite color scheme. One way is to choose a dominant color, a subdominant, and an accent—say mostly yellow, some orange, and just touches of blue.

High style in color schemes is to use different flowers all of the same color—for example, white petunias, lilies, summer phlox, tulips, azaleas, and chrysanthemums. Or you can go the monochromatic route in a slightly different way. Let's say your color is pink. So you select flowers in colors varying from pale pink to dark red. If you like to have plenty of cut flowers for your home, the color scheme outdoors will likely reflect your preference inside.

Color-scheme gardens can also vary around one's house, depending on structural materials and available plants. Here are some suggestions for color-scheme gardens in different seasons:

Yellow-and-white spring garden. For white, the flowers might be appleblossoms, grape-hyacinth, arabis, Dutch hyacinth, clethra, and daffodil. For yellow, tulip, daffodil, basket-of-gold alyssum, coreopsis, and leopard's-bane or doronicum.

Blue-and-white spring garden. For white, the flowers of tulip, dogwood, lily-of-the-valley, and bluets. For blues, the gardener has many choices, but especially crane's-bill geranium, Virginia bluebells, grapehyacinth, periwinkle, lilac, ajuga, iris, mazus, and woods phlox.

Gold-and-yellow late-summer garden. In gold and yellow, black-eyed Susans, early chrysanthemums, and golden-orange marigolds.

Red-and-lavender autumn garden. Red wax begonias (Begonia semperflorens varieties), viburnum berries, hardy asters and chrysanthemums, and mistflower (Eupatorium species).

6•High-Rise Terrace and Rooftop Gardening

Urban gardens, the same as those in the country, need an ample supply of enriched soil to sustain root growth, good light, moisture, and routine attentions to pruning and pest control. The chief difference has to do with our ubiquitous condition—air pollution.

Shrubs and trees known to resist photochemical smog include acacia, aralia, arbutus, boxwood, camellia, cedar, rock-rose, cotoneaster, cypress, ash, ginkgo, plum, pittosporum, pyracantha, oak, spirea, lilac, viburnum, and yucca.

Given a good start, along with moist soil, regular feeding, and thoughtful care, most vegetables, herbs, and flowers show a surprising tolerance for polluted air.

If your garden in the city is earthbound, likely the first thing you will do is clear it of debris, then spade up the soil. Years of soot accumulations don't actually seem to harm soil, but if it has not been regularly cultivated, the surface is often compacted to the point of excluding water and air, both necessary elements for plant growth. Incorporate quantities of peat moss and sand. If you have access to well-rotted manure or compost from the country, so much the better. Getting the top 8'' to 12'' of soil into grow tilth so you can dig in it easily is no small task. However, a lot of effort spent in the beginning on soil preparation will pay off handsomely in vigorous growth for years to come.

For high-rise and rooftop gardens, use fairly large pots—at least 6'' in diameter or more—or planter boxes. Fill with a mix of two parts sand, one part topsoil, and 1 part sphagnum peat moss. Or, if excess weight is a worry, use a mix composed in these proportions: 1/2 bushel of perlite or vermiculite, 1/2 bushel of coarse sphagnum peat moss, four ounces of 20% superphosphate, four ounces of dolomitic limestone, and two ounces of 5-10-5 fertilizer. When plant growth in containers is obviously active, begin feeding every other week with a liquid fertilizer mixed according to label directions.

The greatest problem with plants on high-rise terraces and rooftops is that they dry out rapidly in hot weather. Be prepared to water well at least once a day during hottest weather.

Lack of sunlight is likely to be the main problem with earthbound city gardens, for these are often nestled between tall buildings. The solutions are to prepare the planting beds with special care—and to use shade-loving plants (see page 131).

7•Shade Gardens

If you start by preparing the soil well, and then choose the right plants, a shady garden can be a beautiful place.

Hardy ferns alone can make a shaded space turn into an appealing woodland dell. Best kinds for this purpose include cinnamon, ostrich, interrupted, maidenhair, lady, Christmas, hay-scented, and bracken ferns.

Plants with white, yellow, or pink blossoms, or white-variegated leaves are especially useful in "lighting" shaded areas. Plant white-flowered astilbe, candytuft, lily-of-the-valley, and Hosta subcordata grandiflora. Yellow primroses and daylilies are excellent, also pale pink daylilies and hardy amaryllis (Lycoris squamigera). For variegated foliage, plant selected hostas, varieties of ajuga, and bishop's-weed (Aegopodium podograria).

For large areas of ground cover, as under a grove of trees, consider planting English or Baltic ivies, varieties of Euonymus fortunei, myrtle or periwinkle (Vinca minor), or pachysandra. For early spring bloom, interplant wood hyacinths in the ground cover.

Annuals (or tender perennials treated as annuals) that do well in shaded gardens include everblooming or wax begonias (Begonia semperflorens), bells of Ireland, browallia, coleus, Chinese forget-me-not, balsam, impatiens, lobelia, baby blue eyes, wishbone flower (torenia), annual periwinkle, and viola.

The summer-flowering bulbs represented by caladiums, tuberous-rooted begonias, and achimenes are great choices for color in the shade.

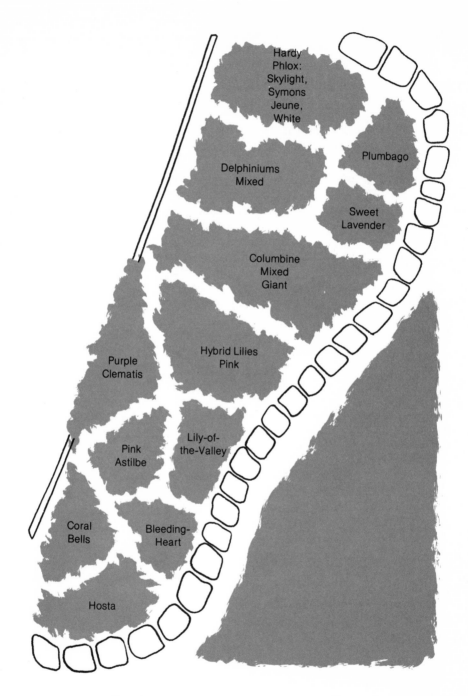

Plan for a perennial garden in partial shade

8•The Gentle Art of Window-Box Gardening

Although window boxes are a part of the outdoor garden, you can propagate certain plants indoors in winter and spring in order to have an abundant supply of window-box-making material in late spring and early summer—or pick up started transplants at your local garden center.

For a sun-drenched window box you could start these plants:

Ageratum
Balsam, Dwarf Bush
Begonia, Wax
Cacti and other succulents
Cockscomb, Dwarf
Dianthus, Dwarf
Geranium
Globe Amaranth, Dwarf

Lantana
Marigold, Dwarf
Petunia, Cascade types
Phlox, Annual
Snapdragon, Dwarf
Verbena, Dwarf Bush
Zinnia, Dwarf

For a window box facing east, or in semishade, these plants are excellent:

Begonia, Wax
Browallia
Coleus
Dusty Miller
Geranium

Lobelia
Petunia, Cascade types
Salvia, Dwarf
Torenia
Vinca

For a window box in full shade, choose from any of the plants listed for semisunny and semishady locations in this book, or any of these which are especially outstanding:

Achimenes
Begonia, Tuberous
Beloperone (Shrimp Plant)
Bromeliads
Caladium
Chlorophytum (Spider Plant)

Cissus
Croton
Fuchsia
Impatiens
Plectranthus
Vinca

You can put small plants directly into a window box filled with a mixture of equal parts soil, sand, and sphagnum peat moss. In the absence of enough rainfall, water frequently to keep soil evenly moist. Large, or permanent-potted plants are best left in their containers, merely set inside the window box with moist peat moss filled in around them. Window box plants need regular feedings of a good, liquid house-plant fertilizer through the summer, and protection from insect invasions. Bring any plants you wish to save indoors before frost.

9•Hanging and Climbing House Plants

Plants that do well in baskets and on trellises are the trapeze artists of the plant world—they are at their best swinging, dangling, or climbing in a window garden. You can use wooden, wire, or plastic hanging baskets (sold locally or by mail), or suspend a small ceramic strawberry jar. Regular clay and plastic flowerpots may be used also, suspended in a handcrafted macrame holder, or by more conventional wire or chain hangers.

Line wooden baskets with plastic film so that soil won't wash through the cracks. Wire and plastic baskets need to be lined first with coarse, unmilled sphagnum moss or florist sheet moss, then filled with soil. Some growers go one step more and give the moss liner a lining of burlap, then add soil and plants.

Culture of hanging-basket plants varies according to the plant. In general, they need evenly-moist soil, good light, and average house warmth. Water by immersing container at sink, or in pail. Allow to soak, then drain so that the basket will not drip when it is returned to the window.

When weather is warm outdoors, hanging baskets do beautifully suspended from house eaves or low-hanging tree branches. Just be sure that drying winds or too much sun don't blister tender leaves or burn up succulent roots.

Good hanging-basket plants, of easy culture under average house or office conditions, include these: trailing begonias, rosary vine, spider plant, lipstick vine (aeschynanthus), cissus, episcia, baby's-tears, hoya, pellionia, philodendron, pilea species, plectranthus (Swedish ivy and other varieties), sedums, and wandering Jew.

House plants for trellises may be divided into two groups—those that climb by tendrils or twining stems, and those that trail naturally but which you can train to climb on some kind of trellis—usually handcrafted to fit the space you have, using slender bamboo plant stakes secured with green plant-ties (with wire embedded).

Climbing plants for indoors include Heavenly Blue morning-glories, black-eyed-Susan vine, creeping gloxinia (Maurania, not a true gloxinia), sweet-potato, gloriosa-lily, dipladenia, passionflower, and climbing nasturtium. All need several hours of sunlight daily in order to grow and flower.

10•Two Ways to Train Plants (And Have a Lot of Fun)

Not since the 16th and 17th centuries have gardeners shown so much interest in training plants to special forms. While the ancient Romans may have spent a lifetime training and clipping boxwood into fanciful animal and geometrical shapes, we create the effect of these almost overnight by covering moss-stuffed wire frames with rooted cuttings of small-leaved English-ivy. Sedate, bushy house plants take on an air of high style when trained as trees or standards, and these same plants can be fashioned into two-dimensional designs or patterns by borrowing from espalier techniques used outdoors.

Our excitement in sculpturing plants as art pieces, and lavishing good culture on them, follows in the wake of a national interest in bonsai. It also indicates that we are maturing as a nation of gardeners. It takes a great deal of patience and understanding of plants to practice the arts of topiary and espalier. Remember, ''As the twig is bent, so grows the branch,'' and as you train plants to make them more decorative, you will discover that this is gardening at its best.

How to Make Almost Instant Topiary

Frames for ''overnight'' topiaries may be formed in almost any shape, but some frequently seen include rabbits, poodles, cranes, and peacocks; balls, cubes, diamonds, and obelisks; and pineapples, mushrooms, and fanciful trees. These are made commercially of stainless steel at prices ranging from $100 to $500 and up for a 6' topiary carousel horse. Fortunately, it is possible to make long-lasting topiary frames inexpensively at home, by using No. 8 or No. 10 galvanized iron wire, available in coils at hardware stores or lumber yards.

Decide on your intended shape and begin the frame by making a spiral which will form the basic body. Next, add ribs of the same wire up and down the back, and legs if needed. Use small strips of masking tape to hold the structure temporarily, then tie permanently with some small wire at all joints. Sometimes it is necessary to cover the form with wire chicken mesh (or florist mesh) to hold moss stuffing well. Small frames can be anchored in the container by extending wire to the bottom and coiling it two or three times, then covering with an inch or two of plaster of Paris. (Avoid sealing drain holes in containers, however.) Larger frames will need containers in suitable proportion or heavy bases, and for these anchoring purposes, concrete may be used. Paint the completed frame work with dark-green enamel.

After the frame is complete and anchored, stuff it tightly with moist, unmilled sphagnum moss. Then you will be ready to plant it thickly with rooted cuttings of English-ivy or creeping fig (Ficus repens). For best results, these should be of uniform size and age. Small-leaved ivies such as Shamrock and Needlepoint are best for small topiaries.

Newly-planted topiaries need to be misted twice daily with water. Keep the moss moist at all times and feed biweekly with a liquid house-plant fertilizer. Trim frequently to shape, and use hairpins to hold wayward strands in place. Ivy will last up to two years when planted this way, the creeping fig even longer, before replanting becomes necessary. Keep these plant sculptures outdoors beside terrace or pool for summer. Winter them in a cool, bright room, or even under fluorescent lights in your basement.

How to Transform House-Plant Bushes Into Stylish Trees

Almost any house plant that normally grows as a bush or shrub can be trained into a tree shape. The standard or tree rose is a good example of this gardening concept. A plant trained in this manner can be used in countless places indoors in any season, and outdoors in the summer in a protected place.

The basic training rules hold for all the plants to be suggested. First, select a young plant with strong tip growth, and be sure that the main growing tip is not harmed. Often a rooted cutting or seedling growing as one stem makes a good choice. Work toward a finished shape that will show a bare trunk topped by a ball, pyramid, cone, or umbrella of leaves and flowers.

Remove all side shoots as soon as they form on the young tree. This encourages the trunk to increase rapidly in height. Leaves, however, that grow along the trunk should be left until the tree has begun to form a terminal framework of leafy branches.

By the time a new tree is 12'' tall it will need to be in a 6'' to 8'' container. This allows room for a bamboo stake high and heavy enough to accommodate the mature tree. Use a soft, plastic plant-tie material to attach the trunk to the stake. Repot whenever roots begin to fill the container. Give proper light, temperature, water, and fertilizer. A sunny location is necessary to develop a straight trunk; indoors, give your tree a quarter turn counter-clockwise each time you water to assure that all parts receive an equal amount of light.

Remove the main growing tip when the trunk has reached the height at which you desire branches to form. Later, pinch out branch tips to improve the tree's shape. From the time branches begin, be sure to turn the tree counter-clockwise a little every time you water so that it can develop symmetrically. Some exciting house-plant "trees" you might try include sweet bay, scented geraniums, heliotrope, lemon-verbena, myrtle, rosemary, sage, santolina, culinary thyme, and coleus.

Some of the Chinese hibiscus make outstanding house-plant trees, and they are nearly everblooming. Varieties recommended for this kind of culture include Brilliant, Kona, Mme. Chiang Kai-shek, President, and White Wings.

Practically any strong-growing hybrid fuchsia, as well as the old-fashioned Gartenmeister Bohnstedt (the honeysuckle fuchsia), can be trained as a tree. Some suggested varieties include Capri, Texas Longhorn, Fort Bragg, Southgate, Troubador, Pink Delight, American Beauty, Flamboyant, and Marinka.

Other house plants that make handsome trees include abutilon, allamanda, aucuba, avocado, azalea, angel-wing begonia, shrimp plant, bougainvillea hybrids, camellia, small-flowered chrysanthemums, dizygotheca, weeping fig, gardenia, geraniums of all kinds, English-ivy hybrids (grafted onto fatshedera standards), pink-polka-dot, lantana, Marguerite daisy, ornamental pepper, royal poinciana, miniature rose, and tibouchina.

Espaliering

The practice of training plants so that they have essentially two dimensions instead of three is called "espaliering." By using No. 9 galvanized wire for the frames, with No. 18 wire for the joints, or redwood for larger designs, it is possible to train certain house plants, trees, and shrubs into any of the classic espalier patterns, or into free-form contemporary designs. Once the basic framework is completed and anchored in a suitable container, or in the garden, all you have to do is add a young plant with pliable stems, remove unnecessary branches and retain those that adapt to the design. Use soft, green, plastic plant-tie material to hold the branches in place.

Herbs, especially myrtle and rosemary, are among the most delightful of plants that can be trained as container-grown espaliers. Other herbs that perform well this way include sweet bay, scented geraniums, lemon-verbena, sage, and santolina. House plants to try as espaliers include almost any with fairly small leaves and reasonably bendable stems, such as trailing or basket-type fuchsias, camellias (especially Showa-No-Sakae, Debutante, Pink Pagoda, Mathotiana Supreme, and Hiryo), weeping fig, coleus, iresine, pellionia, pilea, any dwarf citrus, Fatshedera lizei, plectranthus, and English-ivy.

Espaliered house plants add interest to any setting, but just as important, they also save space. Kinds that would naturally grow into specimens bigger than a bushel can be trained into a flat design or pattern that has height and width, but only 2'' or 3'' of depth. Large espaliers can be highly decorative against a wood-paneled wall, and small ones, perhaps rosemary or ivy trained in a fleur-de-lis pattern, can serve as a living art object on a table or shelf.

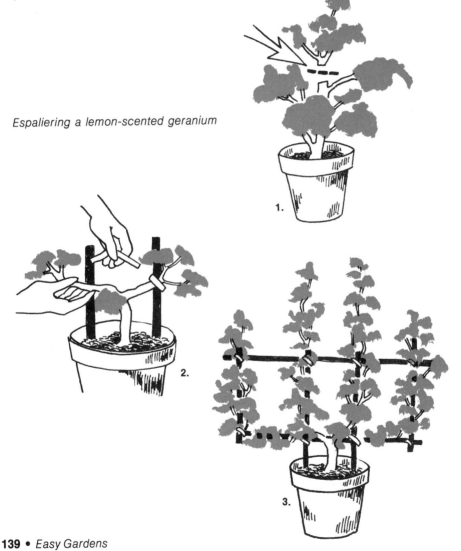

Espaliering a lemon-scented geranium

11•By-Mail Sources for Seeds, Bulbs, and Nursery Stock

Antonelli Brothers, 2545 Capitola Road, Santa Cruz, California 95060. *Tuberous begonias, gloxinias, achimenes, ferns.*

Burgess Seed & Plant Company, 67 East Battle Creek, Galesburg, Michigan 49053. *House plants, bulbs, nursery stock.*

W. Atlee Burpee Company, Warminster, Pennsylvania, 18974. *Seeds, bulbs, supplies and equipment; home greenhouses.*

Farmer Seed and Nursery Company, Inc., Faribault, Minnesota 55021. *House plants, seeds, bulbs, nursery stock.*

Henry Field Seed and Nursery Company, 407 Sycamore, Shenandoah, Iowa, 51601. *House plants, nursery stock, seeds, bulbs, supplies.*

Gurney Seed and Nursery Company, Yankton, South Dakota 57078. *Seeds, bulbs, plants, supplies.*

Jackson & Perkins Company, Medford, Oregon 87501. *Seeds, bulbs, roses, nursery stock.*

Lyndon Lyon, 14 Mutchler Street, Dolgeville, New York 13329. *African violets and other gesneriads; miniature roses.*

Earl May Seed and Nursery Company, Shenandoah, Iowa 51603. *Seeds, bulbs, plants, nursery stock, supplies.*

George W. Park Seed Co., Inc., Greenwood, South Carolina 29647. *Seeds, bulbs, plants, supplies.*

John Scheepers, Inc., 63 Wall Street, New York, New York 10005. *Flowering bulbs for indoors and outdoors.*

Sunny Brook Farms, 9448 Mayfield Road, Chesterland, Ohio 44026. *Herbs, scented geraniums, house plants, sedums, and sempervivums (send 50¢ for catalog).*

Thon's Garden Mums, 4815 Oak Street, Crystal Lake, Illinois 60014. *Chrysanthemums.*

Three Springs Fishers, Lilypons, Maryland 21717. *Water-lilies, lotus, garden pools, pumps, aquatic plants, all kinds of fish for garden pools (send $1 for catalog).*

White Flower Farm, Litchfield, Connecticut 06759. *Perennial flowers, shrubs, and bulbs (send $3.50 for catalog).*

Index

Hoya, 135
Hyacinths, 39, 44, 124, 126, 128, 129, 131
Hydrangea, 61, 72

Ice Plant, 121
Immortelle, 47
Impatiens, 47, 54, 131
Iris, 39, 44, 50, 121, 124, 126, 129
Ivy, 11, 91, 92, 131, 135, 136, 137
Ixia, 44

Jack-in-the-pulpit, 125
Japanese Arrowhead, 124
Japanese Holly, 73, 74
Jasmine, 128
Juniper, 73

Kalanchoe, 54
Kansas Gayfeather, 51

Lagurus, 47
Larkspur, 45, 125
Lavender, 73, 121
Lawns, 30, 85-90
Leopard's-bane, 129
Light, 17-8, 116
Lilac, 72, 126, 128, 130
Lilies, 41, 50, 54, 124, 128, 131
Lily-of-the-valley, 50, 91, 126, 129, 131
Limnanthes, 125
Lipstick Vine, 135
Lobelia, 131
Lycoris, 42, 131

Marble Vine, 81
Marigolds, 33, 45, 121, 129
Mazus, 129
Mignonette, 125, 128
Mistflower, 129
Mock-orange, 72, 126, 128
Moonflowers, 128
Morning-glory, 135
Mountain-laurel, 73
Mulching, 32, 45, 47, 92-3, 106, 112, 113

Nasturtium, 135
Needie, 6, 9, 88

Nepeta mussini, 123
Nicotiana, 48, 125, 128
Nierembergia, 121
Nigella, 125
Night-blooming cereus, 128

Organic gardening, 30-4, 92

Pachysandra, 11, 92, 131
Passionflower, 135
Pearl Everlasting, 47
Pellionia, 135
Penstemon, 121
Peonies, 48, 72, 126
Periwinkle, 11, 121, 129, 131
Petunias, 39, 45, 54, 128
Philodendron, 135
Phlox, 39, 42, 45, 50, 121, 123, 125, 129
Pinks, 121
Pittosporum, 130
Plant
    diseases, 31-3
    pests, 31, 32, 33
Planting
    berries, 111, 113, 115
    flowers, 39-54
    shrubs, 75-8
    trees, 57, 68-70
    vines, 82
Polemonium reptans, 123
Pollination, 97, 106, 109, 114
Poppies, 45, 124, 125
Portulaca, 45
Potpourri, 126-7
Potting Mixes, 117
Primrose, 50, 123, 131
Privet, 74
Pruning
    berries, 114
    fruit trees, 106
    herbs, 101, 102
    shrubs, 74, 78
    trees, 69, 70
    vegetables, 97
    vines, 82
Pulmonaria, 123
Purple Wintercreeper, 91
Pyracantha, 73, 130

Ranunculus, 44
Rhodanthe, 47
Rhododendron, 71
Rock gardens, 121-3
Rock-rose, 130
Rosary Vine, 135
Rose-moss, 42, 121
Roses, 32, 51-2, 127
Rotenone, 33
Rudbeckia, 125
Ryania, 33

Salvia, 45
Saponaria ocymoides, 121, 128
Sedums, 54, 121, 123, 135
Sempervivums, 54, 121, 123
Shrubs, 48, 71-8
Silver Fleece Vine, 83
Snapdragons, 47, 121
Snowball, 72
Snowdrops, 39
Snowflake, 39, 126
Snow-in-summer cerastium, 121
Soil, 28-30, 117
    acidity (pH), 29, 87, 111, 113, 115
Solomon's-seal, 125
Sparaxis, 44
Sphagnum Peat Moss, 29, 69, 75, 86,
    93, 130, 134
Spirea, 71, 130
Spring Beauty, 125
Statice, 47
Sternbergias, 42
Stout, Ruth, 93
Strawflower, 47
Succulents, 52-4, 128
Sun-rose, 121
Sweet Rocket, 128

Thalictrum, 123
Thunbergia alata, 81, 129, 135
Tigridia, 44
Trees
    evergreens, 66-7

flowering, 60-2
for foliage, 62-4
for shade, 55-7
for windbreaks, 65-6
ornamental, 57-60
planting of, 68-9
Trenching, 30
Trichogramma, 32
Trillium, 48, 125
Trumpet Vine, 83
Tuberoses, 44, 128
Tulips, 41, 50, 126, 129

Vegetables, 94-9
Verbenas, 39, 42, 45, 121
Vermiculite, 42
Viburnum carlesi, 126, 128, 129, 130
Vinca minor, 92
Vines, 81-3, 111
Viola, 131
Violets, 125
Virginia Bluebell, 125, 129

Waterer Laburnum, 62
Watsonia, 44
Weed Eater string-line trimmers
    for clearing heavy undergrowth, 12
    for edging, 9
    for mowing, 11
    for scalping, 10-2
    for sweeping, 11
    for trimming, 10, 88, 123
    types and uses of, 14
Weeding, 92
Weed killers, 89
White Snakeroot, 125
Wild Ginger, 91, 125
Wild Strawberry, 91
Witch-hazel, 72

Yew, 74
Yuccas, 54, 130

Zinnias, 45, 125